a face for radio

radio station planning and design

This book is dedicated to our children:
Glenn Barr, Lesley Barr, Jessica Bloomfield,
Gabriel Bloomfield, Corinne Motl and
the electromagnetic spectrum at large.

Acquisitions Editor: Angelina Ward
Publishing Services Manager: André Cuello
Project Manager: André Cuello
Assistant Editor: Doug Shults
Marketing Manager: Christine Degon
Cover Design: Bloomfield & Associates, *Architects*
Book Design: Bloomfield & Associates, *Architects*

Focal Press is an imprint of Elsevier
30 Corporate Drive, Suite 400, Burlington, MA 01803, USA
Linacre House, Jordan Hill, Oxford OX2 8DP, UK

Recognizing the importance of preserving what has been written,
Elsevier prints its books on acid-free paper whenever possible.

Library of Congress Cataloging-in-Publication Data

British Library Cataloguing-in-Publication Data
A catalogue record for this book is available from the British Library.

ISBN 13: 978-0-240-80803-1
ISBN 10: 0-240-80803-7

For information on all Focal Press publications visit our website at
www.books.elsevier.com

07 08 09 10 11   5 4 3 2 1

Printed in China

cover credit:
View From Garlington Road
Entercom Communications
Greenville, South Carolina
Bloomfield & Associates, Architects
Photographer: © *F.Flips*

title page credit:
Concept Section
Entercom Communications
Denver, Colorado
Bloomfield & Associates, Architects

*The National Association of Broadcasters (NAB) is a trade association
that advocates on behalf of more than 8,300 free, local radio and
television stations and broadcast networks before Congress, the
Federal Communications Commission and the Courts.*

a face for radio

radio station planning and design

ON AIR

KOSI
KALC
KOMT
KEZW

Peter **Bloomfield**   *Mark* **Motl**   *Vilma* **Barr**

Early Image of KDKA, c. 1922
The First Commercial Radio Station in the United States
Pittsburgh

KPLU Proposed Studio Rendering, 2006
NPR Station at Pacific Lutheran University
Tacoma

contents

If you're driving into town
With a dark cloud above you
Dial in the number
Who's bound to love you

Oh honey you turn me on
I'm a radio
I'm a country station
I'm a little bit corny
I'm a wildwood flower
Waving for you
Broadcasting tower...

You Turn Me On, I'm A Radio
For the Roses, c.1972
Joni Mitchell

Early Concept Sketch
KPLU at Pacific Lutheran University
Tacoma

The planning and design of the facilities from which radio broadcasts originate is a multi-faceted specialty. It involves architecture, interior design, engineering, and an appreciation of the physical image that the station communicates.

This book was commissioned by the *National Association of Broadcasters* to fulfill two primary objectives. The first is that the professional literature did not include a thorough and practical guide to help radio station management through the process of building or expanding the physical spaces needed to support its format.

Second, the book expands the management and technical aspects of radio by integrating the station's image in the community as expressed by its physical facilities. It includes both the exterior and the interior. The station could occupy all or part of a free-standing structure on a busy highway or street. Or, the station could be located within a multi-purpose structure in a city, a mall, or an office park. Both options often become settings for station-sponsored events where advertisers, community members, elected officials, and talent of all types are invited.

Radio occupies an indelible place in the minds of listeners. All radio is local, all 13,748 licensed stations in the United States. It is a growth industry. In the past six years, the number of licensed radio stations has increased by eight percent. Radio, which reaches ninety-four percent of all consumers every week, is much more intimate than other media.

It goes where its listeners go. They take pride in their radio preferences. It is part of their urban fabric. Radio stations employ many thousands of talented individuals in every segment of a station's operations, from talent to support.

A Face for Radio: Radio Station Planning and Design demonstrates how to implement a facility that relates to the style in which a station's human resources can most productively function. And, it shows how the station's physical facility assumes the role of an asset that influences its bottom line, through a subtle and on-going affirmation of its public image.

David K. Rehr, President and CEO
National Association of Broadcasters
Washington, D.C.

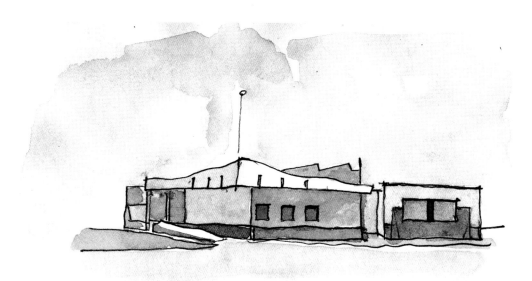

Early Massing Study
Cox Radio
Babylon

preface

A few years ago, I was asked to present a lecture at the annual National Association of Broadcasters Radio Conference on the design of facilities. At that time, my firm had completed a half-dozen projects for stations in various parts of the country. I was pleased to have this opportunity to think about the lessons learned and pass them on to colleagues and clients.

It became clear early on that while explaining issues of organization were critical, doing so without also explaining the role of budget, schedule, the design team, and other aspects of the process would leave voids in the presentation accordingly. I asked to change the format from a lecture to a panel and invited a broadcast engineer, a real estate consultant, and a general manager/client to join the discussion. The turnout and response to the session were excellent.

At about the same time, I began a dialogue with Steven Mitchel, Head Librarian at the NAB. As the industry reference resource, he regularly received inquiries from broadcast facility owners, engineers, and managers for information resources to design and build these facilities. In response to this need, the NAB asked us to develop on a book about the design of broadcast facilities.

It had always been clear to us as architects that while television and radio do occasionally sit under one roof, there is relatively little in common in regard to design. We are pleased to present here the first of two planned books, *A Face for Radio: Radio Station Planning and Design.* The second book on television is in the pipeline.

Peter Bloomfield AIA / NCARB
Bloomfield and Associates, Architects
Philadelphia

Concept Watercolors
Entercom Communications
Denver

acknowledgements

Thank you efforts fall into two categories:

The intangible includes just about everyone who has made our effort interesting, if not easier, as we designed and worked on the construction of broadcast facilities. Good clients make good architecture. They approach a project with an open eye and with both experience and a willingness to disregard their own preconceived ideas. They expect their architects to do the same.

Without these smart, experienced, and considerate men and women-at all levels of the industry, in large markets and small, whether a new building or a small renovation-there would be fewer good buildings and really no need for a book such as this.

Many individuals have been part of making this book tangible. The taking of beginning concepts and converting them into what we hope is a cogent form and format has relied on several significant individuals. Beth Van Why and Lisa Calabro gave their eyes and intellect as the graphic layout continually developed. This book looks and feels as it does due to their diligence.

Many of the diagrams and statistical research were collated by the architects at Bloomfield & Associates, Architects. Their intelligent and careful work over the years has been integral to defining broadcast facilities as they are today.

The engineering, lighting and acoustic consultants were as integral to the making of this book as they are to the making of good facilities. Finally the best in the industry–those managers and engineers who agreed to be interviewed– consistently set a standard of excellence and should be recognized.

Thank You
The Authors

Early Image of KDKA, c. 1922
The First Commercial Radio Station in the United States
Pittsburgh

Equipment Racks
Entercom Communications
Greenville

When the federal government eased regulations on media ownership in 1997, it brought about a spate of consolidation. Fledgling media groups began to merge and acquire stations at a rate never before seen in the United States. Along with the corporate consolidation came the need and interest in developing facilities for this new type of media group.

The opportunity arose to create a physical manifestation of this new business model and to rethink this workplace in general. The architecture of this new model–like the corporate plan itself–has continued to evolve.

The organization of the facility can and should reflect the working style, image, and business goals of the broadcast facility. This applies to the headquarters of all types of radio broadcast organizations, whether a stand-alone station serving small towns, or a consolidated group sharing facilities on the twenty-third floor of a skyscraper in a major metropolitan area. There can never be one way to plan and implement a design for a facility that will best serve the current and future needs of a radio station.

Every station, whether public or private, in a small market or large and independent of format should have its own personality, identifiable by the people who work there and the audience it reaches. The process for devising a satisfying plan for new facilities is both a bubble-up and a trickle-down exercise. With the guidance and expertise of professional consultants, the ideas, visions, and goals of the participants can be realized. And, along with the three-dimensional outcome, will be a perceived pride of ownership.

C-N

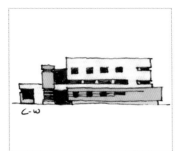

C-W

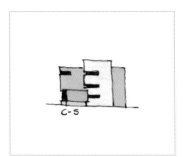

C-S

C-E

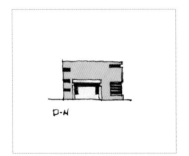

D-N

D-W

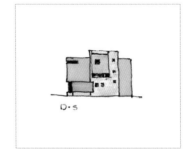

D-S

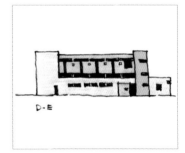

D-E

E-N

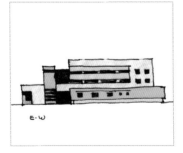

E-W

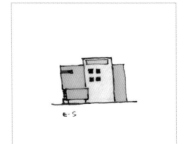

E-S

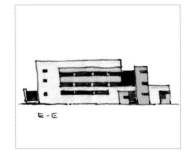

E-E

Massing Options
KPLU at Pacific Lutheran University
Tacoma

chapter one

initiating the process: assembling the team

What are your first steps? You know that something needs to be done for your current facility. It no longer meets all of your needs.

Why?
- You need more space to expand.
- The lease is ending.
- You want to bring multiple stations under one roof.
- The neighborhood has changed and you're looking to relocate.

So, what is involved in the making of a new radio station facility? How can it be done in an organized, affordable, and satisfying manner? The starting point is finding and assembling the right team of staff and professionals who will help form the vision and facilitate the process.

An orderly process is well worth the effort if you are planning to renovate or build a new facility. It also offers the opportunity to create a physical representation of a new business model and to rethink the radio station as a workplace.

It will result in an environment that allows the entire staff to work at their highest level. A facility to help everyone do their jobs best. A facility that helps the promotions department to promote, the sales staff to sell, etc.

Critical to this first step is determining who is best suited to help form that vision and facilitate the process in a way that allows the entire staff to continue doing what they do best: making radio.

Getting Started

It is rare to set an actual starting date for a project. Initially you may have encountered or inherited problems with your facility and you begin speculating on solutions. New staff needs, updated production formats, and changes in technology are the usual instigators. The need to consolidate and upgrade may have been on the horizon for some time. Chances are there have been several quick fixes over time.

These moments of initial speculation will incorporate many and often competing forces, such as short-term vs. long-term costs, engineering requirements, and location opportunities. When these interests are formally drawn together, the team has been formed.

To assure success, the team must establish goals. Some team members will be involved from start to finish; others will have brief but crucial involvement. The structure and dynamics of your team should be carefully considered in relation to the type and scale of the project. The following casting of personalities and roles are a few that you may encounter.

Defining the Needed Roles

While the team's membership and degree of involvement may vary from project to project given the context, size, and management styles, there are a few key members who will be involved throughout the project.

Initially, the team will consist of a few members, typically the general manager, owner, and often the architect. Perhaps there is no more important member than the general manager, representing the end user and responsible for establishing vision and the project's aspirations.

The identity of the owner is project-specific but is often a corporation or institution. Their role is principally project stewardship to assure that prevailing values, goals, and standards are understood and deployed.

The architect is usually the first consultant brought on board and, at this early time, their role is primarily advisory. They work to identify opportunities, outline constraints, and establish means.

Together, this team works to outline basic project parameters. During these initial meetings, there are often more questions than answers, but with input from supporting members, the team develops potential solutions.

There may be no greater contributor to the project team than the existing facility itself. This silent and often overlooked member may be the object of deserved criticism, but it does hold some of the most valuable lessons and should be carefully considered.

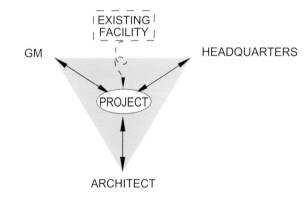

Initial Team Diagram
Bloomfield & Associates, Architects

The Planning Team and The Process

Feasibility Study

The initial step in the process, along with some site considerations, is often the Feasibility Study. The team is expanded to include members who will provide valuable input, and the structure may well resemble the diagram to the right.

Good ideas emanate from a myriad of places. Participation by key staff allows them to embrace the process by encouraging participation–even in the most oligarchical of organizations. The question is: "When and who do you bring into the process?"

The Feasibility Study is a good opportunity for the architect to meet with the department heads and staff to review existing conditions, critique and discuss their work environment, and identify specific requirements. "We need this, not that", "This no longer works" and "I never understood that", are common descriptions. One goal of the study is to establish specific design requirements, what is needed, and how the space will be used.

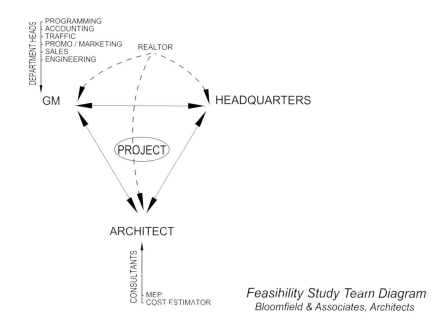

Feasibility Study Team Diagram
Bloomfield & Associates, Architects

The document describing these requirements is commonly referred to as the "Building Program" and is translated into the space types, sizes, and adjacencies by the architect for team review.

When relocation is the task at hand, the real estate agent is the unique member to this phase. Initially, they will work to find viable options that will fulfill requirements.

Accommodating the building program is the principal objective, "Will we fit and how does it work?" The lease/purchase options and associated improvement costs are typically the deciding factors. The feasibility study is a seminal project defining moment. The careful review of the opportunities and constraints that each scheme/site presents is essential to the process. Chapter 2 looks at this component in greater detail.

Design Phase

With a site secured and goals established, the design phase is the next step. As indicated in the diagram to the right, the team will expand to include design professionals whose qualifications assure a successful project. This newly formed component is commonly referred to as the design team.

The architect usually leads this team and is charged with designing and specifying work required to realize the facility. Together with their consultants and their fields of expertise, they can develop solutions in response to the opportunities and constraints outlined in the feasibility study.

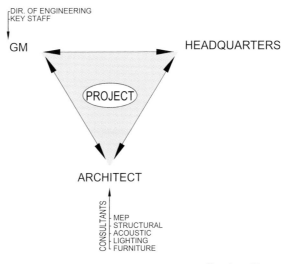

Design Phase Team Diagram
Bloomfield & Associates, Architects

During the initial steps, preliminary drawings and supporting narratives are prepared and presented. There will be numerous meetings to review the progress of the design. Some meetings will address the overall facility while others focus on specific broadcast and operational items.

Team Work Space
Entercom Communications
Kansas City

a face for radio

It is also common for the design team to prepare discrete studies and design options for specific aspects of the project. The impact of these options on the overall project should be carefully considered by the team.

Decisions will have to be made to advance the process, and input from team members is crucial at this step. During productive design review sessions, a significant amount of information will be presented. Some information you may be familiar with, while other aspects appear foreign, especially when navigating the sea of acronyms.

All will take time to digest. You may find yourself thinking things through and approaching it from another point of view. There will typically be a few lingering questions.

Experienced design professionals understand this; they realize the gravity of the task at hand and work to provide the necessary information. *If you don't understand something, ask.*

It is far more effective to make an informed decision during the design phase than leave room for doubt and correction during construction.

The design process is only as informed as the questions asked. Your design team should work hard to ask the right questions and develop viable solutions. This is a brief overview of the design process, and related topics are developed elsewhere in this edition. The team's structure and paths of communication can take several forms and, for the most part, are project-specific. However you can anticipate a similar casting of roles for the design phase as indicated in the diagram on page 5.

Members of Your Staff

The selection of the right staff members is critical to defining a great project. It is important to identify key staff that will be available to answer questions and review the design process. It is also beneficial to establish one of these people as the point of contact. This can facilitate effective communication with other team members while preserving your staff resources to do their day-to-day jobs.

General Manager
The General Manager is perhaps the most important team member, establishing the vision and aspirations for the project. They best understand the community within which they operate and how their business and broadcast models are developed to interact with the public at large. From the big picture through the details, their consistent involvement throughout the process is invaluable.

Department Managers/Heads
This usually includes managers for the Programming, Sales, Development, Traffic, Promotions, and Accounting departments. Each manager has valuable insight into their daily operations and what improvements would increase productivity.

They should know their staffing needs and any special requirements. These typically include meeting frequencies and sizes, delivery and storage requirements, preferred departmental adjacencies as well as access, and security requirements.

Director of Engineering
The impact of engineering on immediate and long term costs and ease of accommodating the move cannot be overemphasized. The primary role of the Director of Engineering (D of E) is the design and specification of broadcast equipment. The D of E works closely with the design team to assure that all has been accommodated. While predominantly focused on the studios, integration, and technical operations center, the D of E's role is occasionally expanded to include IT, phone, and security systems.

Interested Staff Members

People feel more connected to projects with which they are directly involved in the development. Staff members who are interested in taking part in the planning process offer valuable insight into important needs and desires of which managers are often unaware.

Controller/Head of Accounting

Involving the people that control the budget can potentially speed up the project.

Representative from Headquarters

Is your organization part of a larger infrastructure, corporation, or institution? Typically, a member of the corporate Real Estate and/or Legal Department would participate in the initial discussions to help keep the focus on the corporate approach to a major renovation or new construction undertaking.

KYW Concept Sketches
CBS Radio
Philadelphia

Consulting Professionals

Retaining the right professional team, from the outset can make your job a lot easier. Experience indicates this will lead to a better end-product. The more you hire out, the more your staff can focus on their current work. It is rarely cost-effective to do the planning, design and engineering in-house.

The following list describes the majority of consultants usually retained for a radio station project. Other specialists may be needed per specific needs, dependant upon the scope of the project.

- Architect
- Engineer
  - MEP
    (Mechanical, Electrical & Plumbing)
  - HVAC
    (Heating, Ventilation, & Air Conditioning)
  - Structural
- Consultants
  - Acoustic
  - Lighting
  - Furniture
- Real Estate Broker

Meeting with Key Staff
KPLU at Pacific Lutheran University
Tacoma

Architect

The architect should be hired early on in the process to determine space needs and to help coordinate questions and issues of zoning and general site suitability. It is common practice to interview qualified architects prior to retaining one for the project. The ability to fully understand and coordinate all aspects of the project–from site selection, budget development, and technical needs to finish selections and construction coordination–is critical.

While direct experience with the broadcast industry is not absolutely imperative, it certainly helps to have a professional with a background in problem solving of this type, as the team considers a variety of locations, financing, and scope of construction options.

Engineers - MEP, HVAC, Structural

The engineering consultants make the building's systems work. The station must support induced loads, be cool in the summer, warm in the winter, and have enough electricity to meet operational demands. When moving the station is the task at hand, the consulting engineers may be involved early to evaluate the potential site's existing systems. Their input will identify problems, verify opportunities, and confirm the viability of each option. Chapter 8 looks into this in greater depth.

During the design phase, having engineers with broadcast facilities experience is a plus. However, the project may also be well-served with professional engineers who are experienced with the specific technical tasks at hand.

Acoustical Consultant

Studio sound quality is crucial to your project, and hiring a consultant with this expertise is essential. When considering a new site in close proximity to a noise source (planes, trains, and automobiles), the acoustical consultant will often make preliminary recommendations that address sound source and attenuation issues. During the design phase, their role often includes establishing the acoustical design criteria, ambient sound levels, and the design of attenuation assemblies. (Please see Chapter 8.) When interviewing acoustical consultants, experience is the priority. Typically the architect coordinates this aspect of the project.

Lighting Consultant

Lighting fundamentally establishes how the station is perceived. Whether illuminating an office, studio, or the exterior of your facility, *the lighting should be effective, dramatic, and efficient to operate.* The lighting consultant should carefully consider who will be occupying the space, how it will be used, and for what period of time. They should also have a good working knowledge of lighting products, controls, and the willingness to prepare options that balance aesthetic, maintenance, and operational concerns which stick to the budget.

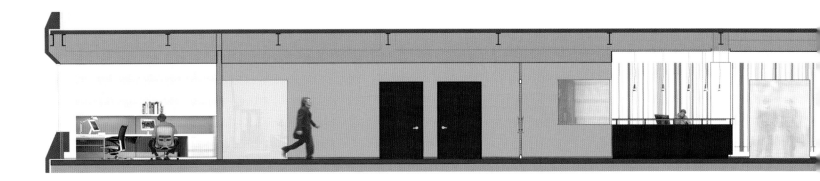

Furniture Consultant

The furniture consultant provides several key services to the project. Initially they survey and evaluate existing furnishings. The typical categories are what should be re-used or re-furbished, and which furnishings are well beyond their life expectancy. Working with other team members, this information is incorporated into the furniture design and the overall budget.

Apart from generating and administering furniture specifications and proposals, one of their most important roles is establishing what goes where, and orchestrating move-in day.

Real Estate Broker

The real estate broker is responsible for identifying location options within the market. Their task is to set out opportunities–buildings, sites, comparative costs–that satisfy the requirements established by the project team.

Typically their fees are paid by the landlord or seller as a percentage of the total deal. Other payment options include hiring the Real Estate Broker on a fixed-fee or hourly basis.

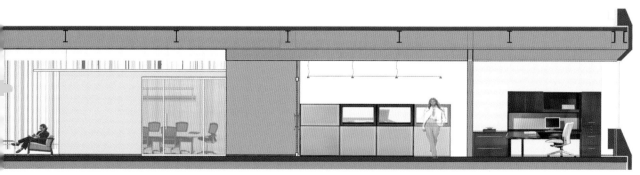

WYSP Rendering
CBS Radio
Philadelphia

Design and Photo Credits

p ii   Early Image of KDKA, c. 1922
KDKA
Pittsburgh, Pennsylvania
Source: KDKA Archives

KPLU Proposed Studio Rendering
KPLU at Pacific Lutheran University
Tacoma, Washington
Source: Bloomfield & Associates, Architects

p iv   Early Concept Sketch
KPLU at Pacific Lutheran University
Tacoma, Washington
Source: Bloomfield & Associates, Architects

p vi   Early Massing Study
Cox Radio
Babylon, New York
Source: Bloomfield & Associates, Architects

p viii   Concept Watercolors
Entercom Communications
Denver, Colorado
Source: Bloomfield & Associates, Architects

p x   Early Image of KDKA, c. 1922
KDKA
Pittsburgh, Pennsylvania
Source: KDKA Archives

Equipment Racks
Entercom Communications
Greenville, South Carolina
Source: Bloomfield & Associates, Architects

p xii   Massing Options
KPLU at Pacific Lutheran University
Tacoma, Washington
Source: Bloomfield & Associates, Architects

p 6   Team Work Space
Entercom Communications
Kansas City, Kansas
Source: Bloomfield & Associates, Architects
Photographer: © Stephen Swalwell

p 9   KYW Concept Sketches
CBS Radio
Philadelphia, Pennsylvania
Source: Bloomfield & Associates, Architects

p 10   Meeting with Key Staff
KPLU at Pacific Lutheran University
Tacoma, Washington
Source: Bloomfield & Associates, Architects

p 12-13   WYSP Rendering
CBS Radio
Philadelphia, Pennsylvania
Source: Bloomfield & Associates, Architects

Typical Project Phases

- Project Definition
    - A. Program Development (see Chapter 2)
    - B. Site Selection (Stay or Move, Chapter 3)
    - C. Initial Budget (see Chapter 5)
    - D. Schedule (see Chapter 8)
- Project Design
    - A. Schematic Design
      The initial design phase, introduces a variety of design ideas; schemes are explored.
    - B. Design Development
      Once a design direction is selected, the phase further develops the design to a more detailed level.
    - C. Construction Documents
      The development of drawings and documents for construction, implementing code requirements, wall details, etc.
- Bidding and Construction
- Move-in

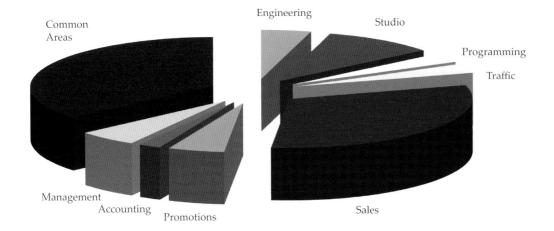

Common
Areas

Engineering

Studio

Programming

Traffic

Management

Accounting

Promotions

Sales

Space Allocation Study
Medium Size Commercial Station
Bloomfield & Associates, Architects

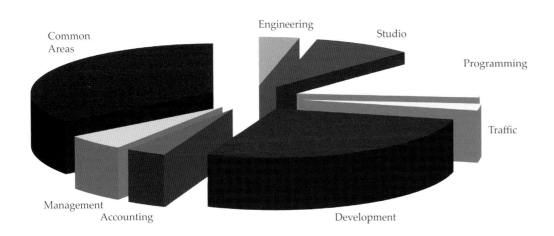

Common
Areas

Engineering

Studio

Programming

Traffic

Management

Accounting

Development

Space Allocation Study
Academic / Public Radio Station
Bloomfield & Associates, Architects

chapter two

program development

A design program for a broadcast facility is not very different from the playbill for a theatrical performance or the program for a sporting event. Both provide information about the participants and the sequence of events. In the case of an architectural or other building design project, the program is a document that includes space needs and other important data pertaining to every aspect of the proposed facility. In addition to listing each individual space, it will often include notes and diagrams about the relationship between various departments, individuals, or service groups.

This inventory of individual needs typically carries with it specific square footage requirements. One program director may need an office of about 130 square feet for meeting with representatives of the music industry. Another program director may only need a work station or access to an enclosed room where a morning show staff can gather as a group before and after being on air.

A local sales manager may need direct access to the sales associates with enough office space to accommodate three people. On the other hand, a national sales manager, typically, has limited exposure to the sales staff, and rarely has meetings in their office. Close access to the general manager, however, is often required. Your architect will analyze these and similar issues with the staff to develop appropriate solutions.

Determining Your Space Needs

Chances are that the stations have been operating in a working environment that performs adequately in some ways and doesn't in others. When a new station is constructed or the existing facility is significantly renovated, the design can impact how your staff members perform and how the station interacts with the community at-large. *Ultimately, the design will affect the bottom line.*

While there are typical requirements for most job descriptions, each vary with locale, format, size of the facility, and individual job description. Station management should take this opportunity to compare responsibilities of both professional and support staff, and review how well the environment supports their activities. Typically, there will be areas–both tangible and intangible–that will be identified for improvement.

Tangible vs Intangible

Tangible elements include such items as specific office and studio sizes as well as hallways and other circulation elements. Support spaces such as toilet rooms, mechanical and electrical rooms, and storage space are also items that must be accounted for in the design.

Intangible elements are areas sometimes referred to as "extra," "public," or "shared" spaces that may in fact serve useful purposes. They can be transformed to function as supplementary meeting places or informal gathering areas that foster communication between staff members. Areas that fall into this category include the lobby, kitchen, and conversation niches in hallways. Or, they can assume a role as visually supportive of the station's public image. Either way, they are an accepted part of the practice of contemporary facility design and have proven to be popular and effective.

Typical Office Areas

Office size and location should be based on task and job needs rather than the status of the occupant. A local sales manager, for example, typically needs to have meetings with 2-3 people. Depending on station format, a program director could handle the work flow in an open work station created with sound-absorbent, tack-up panels. Or, a larger enclosed office with more privacy may be required.

Often, shared spaces can satisfy the need for shared tasks and solutions. This option, for example, can be applied to members of the station's traffic and promotion departments.

Type	Department	Subtotal	Circ.	Total
	1. Programming			
By Station		765	370	1126
	2. Studio			
By Station		3500	1715	5215
	3. Promotions			
By Station		1182	579	1761
	4. Traffic			
Shared		909	445	1354
	5. Engineering			
Shared		1101	539	1640
	6. Management			
Shared		1335	654	1989
	7. Accounting			
Shared		519	254	773
	8. Sales			
By Station		6124	3001	9125
	9. Common Areas			
Shared		2989	1465	4454
	TOTALS	18,415	9,023	27,437

Typical Programming Summary
Bloomfield & Associates, Architects

Department	Position	Off. Size (Sq. Ft.)	Off. Size (Nom. Dim)	No. of Spaces	Subtotal	Circ.	Total
1. Programming	See Individual Stations						
2. Studio	See Individual Stations						
	Group "A"						
Studio	On Air	270	15 x 18	2	540	540	702.00
Studio	Control Production	160	10 x 16	2	320	320	416.00
Support	Morning Show/Jock Prep	255	15 x 15	1	255	255	301.50
	Group "B"						
Studio	On Air	270	15 x 18	3	810	810	1053.00
Studio	Control Production	160	10 x 16	2	320	320	416.00
Support	Morning Show/Jock Prep	255	15 x 15	1	255	255	301.50
3. Promotions							
Office	Mkt. Mgr.	120	10 x 12	1	120	120	156.00
Office	Promo Mgr.	120	10 x 12	1	120	120	156.00
Office	Director	81	9 x 9	2	162	162	210.60
Open Office	Staff/Interns	25	5 x 5	8	200	200	260.00
Support	Storage (small)	40	5 x 8	2	80	80	104.00
Support	Storage (large)	200	10 x 20	2	400	400	520.00
Support	Prize Closet	100	10 x 10	1	100	100	130.00

Space allocation is an important step in designing your new facility. Take into account all current positions and plan for future growth.

Note the Circulation category. This coefficient is needed to provide usable circulation space within the facility.

Typical Programming Summary: Expanded
  Bloomfield & Associates, Architects

Office Space Allocation Guidelines

Senior Management

Typically, offices for the general manager, marketing manager, and controllers should be large enough to handle small meetings, depending on the station's management style. For the general manager, formal meetings might take place at a table in the office. Less formal meetings can be accommodated with visitors occupying one or two chairs in front of the manager's desk, or by utilizing a couch and a chair for the manager. Close access to a conference room could reduce the size of the manager's private office.

The senior management category may also include directors of programming, engineering, and operations. These offices should be sized based on the occupant's specific needs for work surface, filing, storage, and discussion spaces.

Sales

Because of privacy issues relating to strategy implementation, sales managers are typically housed in closed offices. The general sales manager's office should be large enough to accommodate a four-person meeting. In the local sales manager's office, two guest chairs typically fit comfortably.

Theoretically, sales representatives are most productive when they are out calling on advertisers and prospects, and should spend a minimum amount of time in the office. Work stations are commonly appropriated to the sales representatives for such tasks as making phone calls and completing the requisite paper work.

Employees who are assigned to assist sales managers and associates–secretaries and graphic specialists–need a dedicated work area to produce sales and marketing materials, complete with printing, duplicating, collating, and binding machines.

Senior Management and Sales Offices

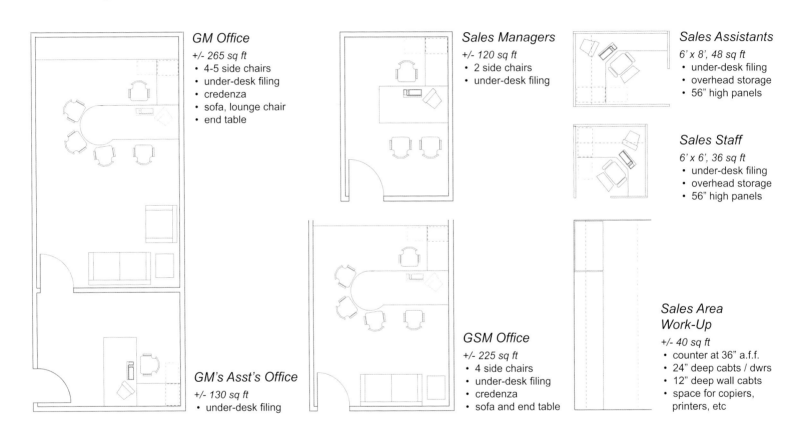

GM Office

+/- 265 sq ft
- 4-5 side chairs
- under-desk filing
- credenza
- sofa, lounge chair
- end table

Sales Managers

+/- 120 sq ft
- 2 side chairs
- under-desk filing

Sales Assistants

6' x 8', 48 sq ft
- under-desk filing
- overhead storage
- 56" high panels

Sales Staff

6' x 6', 36 sq ft
- under-desk filing
- overhead storage
- 56" high panels

GM's Asst's Office

+/- 130 sq ft
- under-desk filing

GSM Office

+/- 225 sq ft
- 4 side chairs
- under-desk filing
- credenza
- sofa and end table

Sales Area Work-Up

+/- 40 sq ft
- counter at 36" a.f.f.
- 24" deep cabts / dwrs
- 12" deep wall cabts
- space for copiers, printers, etc

Typical Space Diagrams
Bloomfield & Associates, Architects

Sales Area Rendering
Entercom Communications
Kansas City

Promotions

The Promotions Department can be situated in a variety of locations with these factors taken into account:

- Secure storage in the Promotion Director's office, with limited access and/or in a locked closet in the promotions area.

- A large and secure area, which may be remote from the station if it is in a high-rent district, for bulky items – *i.e.*, hats, cases of soft drinks or water, CD's, tee shirts, etc.

- Prize room storage, which can be located near the main entry lobby for ease of distribution.

- Packaging or other preparation of giveaway items can be carried out at a long counter or other work surface in the storage area.

Traffic

If Engineering is the station's link to the world, then the Traffic Department is the link between Sales and Programming. They are responsible for the continuity and confirmation of air-time for the station's programs and advertisements.

The location of the Traffic Department is a matter of individual preference at many stations. It is not uncommon to locate the traffic section near accounting, next to sales, or in some situations, near programming. Wherever they are placed, they need lockable storage space for required logs and associated records. With the advent of computerized and Internet-based traffic systems, storage and printing needs have been reduced dramatically over the last 10 years.

Accounting

The broadcast facility's Accounting Department is not unlike other businesses. Along with managing accounts receivable and payable, there are unique accounting methods for the public and private station. When considering a significant move or renovation, this is a good opportunity to review your department's staff and space use requirements.

The Accounting Department often includes private offices for the controller and/or the business manager with enough space for small meetings. These are usually located in close proximity to an open office for departmental staff. The programming process should also review the facility's long and short term file storage as well as the applicability for paper and electronic formats. Paper files have a habit of accumulating and this may be a good time to purge obsolete files prior to establishing how much storage space will be required.

Traffic /Accounting Department Offices

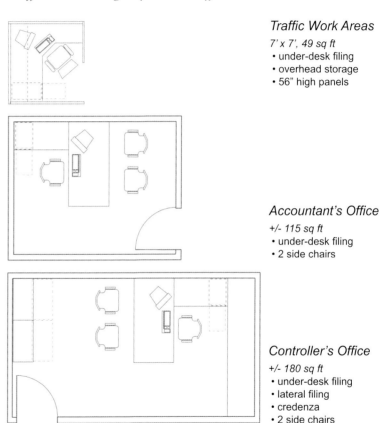

Traffic Work Areas
7' x 7', 49 sq ft
- under-desk filing
- overhead storage
- 56" high panels

Accountant's Office
+/- 115 sq ft
- under-desk filing
- 2 side chairs

Controller's Office
+/- 180 sq ft
- under-desk filing
- lateral filing
- credenza
- 2 side chairs

Typical Space Diagrams
Bloomfield & Associates, Architects

Studio Space Allocation Guidelines

Studios

Planning for the studios–the station's technical soul–is most successful when it is a collaborative effort between programming, production, and engineering. Participants during the planning phase should consider the opportunity to make studios a focus of the theatrical aspect of the facility. Additional costs for such items as additional soundproofing, engineering requirements, and ballistic glazing would be figured into the budget estimate. A facility with multiple formats would also need to decide which stations are "showcased."

Performance Studios

A studio for presentations by visiting performers or for local talent generates positive public relations for the station. This studio is usually located adjacent to the lobby to accommodate pre- and post-production events. It is also a good idea to fit-out the performance studio with the necessary equipment to support additional uses such as a back-up air studio or production studio.

Programming and Production

The amount of space assigned to programming and production will vary based on the station's location, size, and format, but there are some common elements.

On-air talents need computer access and a small area to store personal items. There is often a need for an office for the program director as well as specialty program offices, such as the staff for morning shows. Unless additional space is available, studios often become the work space for the production staff.

With the advent of current broadcast equipment such as routers and electronic storage systems, studios can become interchangeable. This versatility, if managed correctly, can greatly reduce the time when studios are not in use, or can help justify the reduction of overall studio number.

Control Room

Clear Channel Communications
Indianapolis

Performance and Session Studios

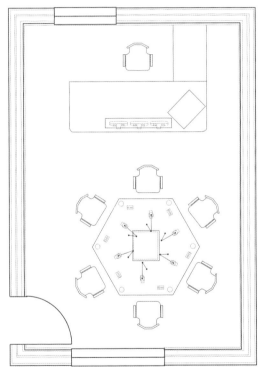

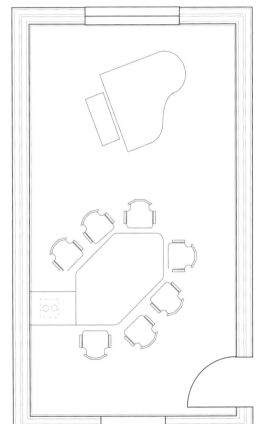

On-Air Studio

+/- 285 sq ft
- seating for 6
- in-studio production

Session Studio

+/- 300 sq ft
- seating for 7
- recording equipment
- performance equipment
- in-house piano

Typical Space Diagrams
  Bloomfield & Associates, Architects

Session Studio
Cox Radio
Birmingham

Production, News Studios and Associated

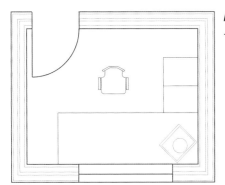

Production Studio

+/- 95 sq ft
• 30" high work counter

News Desk

+/- 115 sq ft
• 30" high work top
• 42" high transaction top

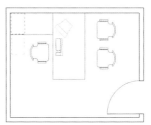

News Director / Expansion Office

+/- 100 sq ft
• under-desk filing
• 2 side chairs

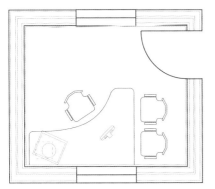

News Studio

+/- 95 sq ft
• 30" high work counter
• 2 guest chairs

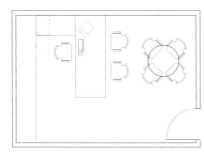

Program Director's Office

+/- 225 sq ft
• under-desk filing
• credenza
• 2 side chairs
• conference table, 4 chairs

Typical Space Diagrams
  Bloomfield & Associates, Architects

Configurations and fit-out of studios are predominantly established by the station's specific broadcast format. This includes the host and guest(s) use requirements as well as sight lines between adjoining studios, and general circulation and access to equipment.

Air Studio
Entercom Communications
Boston

Engineering Space Allocation Guidelines

Engineering

The Engineering Department is the station's electronic hub and its link to the rest of the world. Work space allocations for the engineering staff are based, like spaces for all other departments that are involved with a successful station's operation, on job-related responsibilities and the carrying out of day-to-day tasks. A typical engineering staff will have a hierarchy of office space requirements. These range from private offices with meeting space for the director or market engineer, to work benches for technicians.

The space that is allocated to house the station's engineering department is divided into two distinct areas:

- The high-tech area containing equipment racks, computers, and punch blocks.

- Office and work spaces for the engineering manager and assistant engineers on staff.

To allow for easy access between the technical area and the offices, the engineering department is often located near the studios.

The TOC (Technical Operations Center), also referred to as the Rack Room, is directly connected to all departments within the station.

The Engineering Department should, early in the programming process, be able to estimate the amount of technical space that will be needed to serve the new facility, with a percentage component for future growth. Because much of the engineering equipment can be housed in a system of racks, the number of racks plus circulation space is often an initial determinant of space needs.

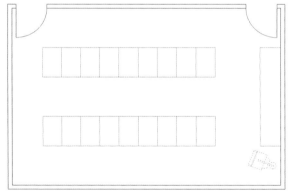

Rack Room
+/- 465 sq ft
- 18 racks
- 36" high work counter
- TV monitor

Typical Space Diagrams
Bloomfield & Associates, Architects

Engineering TOC
Entercom Communications
Kansas City

Support Space Allocation Guidelines

Lobby

The space needs for this area vary greatly, depending on security, the amount of traffic coming through the lobby, and whether the space is part of internal circulation. The receptionist's space, depending on facility size, rarely does a single job. Other secretarial duties include answering the phone and directing calls. In very large stations, reception duties are often handled by more than one person.

Other tasks that are carried out in the lobby's general vicinity include prize distribution as well as mail sorting and distribution (the mail room is typically close by).

Conference Rooms

In many of today's facilities, conference rooms also double as training rooms for sales personnel. Every facility should have space that can comfortably handle a stand-up gathering of the entire staff for announcements. Major all-staff meetings may be best handled off-site.

Mail and Copy Room

With the advent of more affordable and sophisticated printing and copying equipment, centralized copy rooms are disappearing.

Mail rooms typically have pigeon holes for distribution of mail, sorted by individuals or by department. Adequate space should be allowed for postage meters, scales, box and envelope storage, mailing supplies, and a work table.

Storage for Outerwear, Umbrellas, & Similar Items

The space need will vary by region, size of the facility, and whether it is part of a large building or an independent structure.

Toilet Facilities

Minimal space allocations are usually set by building codes and are based on a percentage of square feet and type of use. Some facilities may also require a rest room in close proximity to the studios and be equipped with an audio or intercom system that plays the live broadcast.

Kitchen / Dining

Kitchen services can be situated in one single area, or in individual areas around the station. Coffee bars and vending services can be placed near studios. Remember that facilities located in urban or densely settled suburban areas tend to require smaller kitchens than those located in more remote areas.

The kitchen/dining area, if located and designed correctly, can double as an informal gathering space. Here, the materials selected should be durable and present a clean, warm, and inviting environment. The lighting, furniture, and color palette should emphasize this dual use.

Vehicle Storage

Studies show that in some locales which experience extreme weather (heat or cold), or are crime-prone, it is cost-effective to build or lease garage space to save wear-and-tear on vehicles. This would entail a separate parking structure in close proximity, or garage area within the main building.

Break Area
Cox Radio
Orlando

Conference Rooms

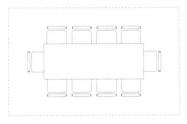

Meeting Area
+/- 185 sq ft
- conference table
- 10 chairs

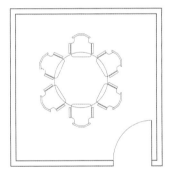

Small Conference
+/- 125 sq ft
- conference table
- 6 conference chairs

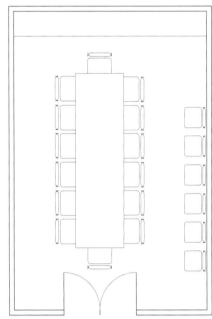

Main Conference
+/- 385 sq ft
- conference table
- 14 conference chairs
- 8 guest chairs

Typical Space Diagrams
  Bloomfield & Associates, Architects

Depending on the value of the real estate where the station is located, it may be more cost-effective to go off-site for staff training purposes. Otherwise, a multi-purpose room can be fitted for audio and visual equipment needed to carry out the training sessions.

Conference Room
Cox Radio
Jacksonville

Space Allocation Comparisons

The space use allocation chart to the right, should be used as a general guide to evaluate or establish the space use requirements for your facility. With any specific project, there will be special considerations and they should be identified early on in the planning process.

The pie chart represents broadcast facilities of varying sizes. For the most part, the space use allocations are proportional between facilities. However, variations are attributable to the economy of scale and specific programmatic requirements associated with stations of

	1 - 2 stations 4 - 7 studios 9,000 - 15,000 net sq ft	3 - 4 stations 8 - 13 studios 14,000 - 27,000 net sq ft	5 - 8 stations 15 - 24 studios 26,000 - 38,000 net sq ft
studios	8.1%	14.4%	14.7%
engineering (TOC)	3.9%	3.2%	2.9%
private offices	25.9%	23.6%	21.0%
open offices	12.0%	13.6%	18.8%
conference / training	8.6%	5.1%	5.5%
lobby	6.3%	3.9%	2.5%
support	10.3%	13.1%	12.0%
circulation	24.9%	23.1%	22.6%
	100.0%	100.0%	100.0%

Percentage of Space Usage
Bloomfield & Associates, Architects

'Private Offices' and 'Open Offices' as shown here include Administrative, Programming, and Sales departments.

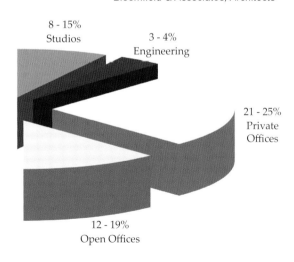

22 - 25%
Circulation

8 - 15%
Studios

3 - 4%
Engineering

10 - 13%
Support

21 - 25%
Private
Offices

2 - 6%
Lobby

5 - 9%
Conference /
Training

12 - 19%
Open Offices

Space Use Allocation Chart
Average of Commercial Stations
Bloomfield & Associates, Architects

Hallways can do more than provide internal walkways to get people from one part of the facility to another. Widening the halls at intervals offers a natural invitation for people to take a few minutes to converse with their colleagues and exchange information. Some of these informal interaction areas are fitted with wall-hung writing boards. The hallway is also a good location for files.

Hallway
Entercom Communications
Boston

Design and Photo Credits

p 23   Sales Area Rendering
        Entercom Communications
        Kansas City, Kansas
        Source: Bloomfield & Associates, Architects

p 27   Control Room
        Clear Channel Communications
        Indianapolis, Indiana
        Source: Luckett & Farley, Architects & Engineers
        Photographer: Willie Allen Productions, AR

p 29   Session Studio
        Cox Radio
        Birmingham, Alabama
        Source: Bloomfield & Associates, Architects

p 31   Air Studio
        Entercom Communications
        Boston, Massachusetts
        Source: Bloomfield & Associates, Architects

p 33   Engineering TOC
        Entercom Communications
        Kansas City, Kansas
        Source: Bloomfield & Associates, Architects
        Photographer: © Stephen Swalwell

p 35   Break Area
        Cox Radio
        Orlando, Florida
        Source: Bloomfield & Associates, Architects

p 37   Conference Room
        Cox Radio
        Jacksonville, Florida
        Source: Bloomfield & Associates, Architects

p 39   Hallway
        Entercom Communications
        Boston, Massachusetts
        Source: Bloomfield & Associates, Architects

Ask these questions in preparation for meeting with your architect.

- At present, is the ratio of private office/shared offices/open workstations correct for the way you would like your department to run?

- What are the meeting types and how many people are in attendance?

- Do you require private conference spaces, open meeting spaces, or both?

- How often does the entire department meet?

- Does your department have any spatial needs which are not currently being addressed? For example: offices, meeting spaces, copy area, etc?

- Which spaces (if any) within your department should be visible to members of the public on a tour of the facility?

- Do any areas (or the whole department) need to be secured from the rest of the facility:
    Outside of regular office hours?
    At all times?

- Do you have sufficient storage in your department?

- What do you need to store?
    Long term?
    Short term?

- Is your department fully staffed at present? If not, how many more staff are you expecting to hire?

- How many staff members do you envision having in each department:
    In five years time?
    In ten years time?

- Which other departments do you interact with regularly?

- Ideally, which department would you like to be adjacent to?

- Does your department need to be close to a public entrance and reception area?

- Does your department require any special equipment, for example: lighting, TV, VCR, secure storage, etc?

Technically Put:

(a) Except for those stations described in paragraph (b) of this section, each AM, FM, and TV broadcast station shall maintain a main studio at one of the following locations:

(1) within the station's community of license;

(2) at any location within the principal community contour of any AM, FM, or TV broadcast station licensed to the station's community of license; or

(3) within twenty-five miles from the reference coordinates of the center of its community of license as described in §73.208(a)(1).

NOTE to paragraph (a): The principal community contour of AM stations that simulcast on a frequency in the 535-1605 kHz band and on a frequency in the 1605-1705 kHz band shall be the 5 mV/m contour of the lower band operation during the term of the simultaneous operating authority. Upon termination of the 535-1605 kHz band portion of the dual frequency operation, the principal community contour shall become the 5 mV/m of the remaining operation in the 1605-1705 kHz band.

(b) The following stations are not required to maintain their main studio at the locations described in paragraph (a) of this section.

(1) AM stations licensed as synchronous amplifier transmitters ("AM boosters") or,

(2) AM, FM, or TV stations, when good cause exists for locating the main studio at a location other than that described in paragraph (a) of this section, and when so doing would be consistent with the operation of the station in the public interest.

(c) Each Class A television station shall maintain a main studio at a location within the station's predicted Grade B contour, as defined in §73.683 and calculated using the method specified in §73.684. With respect to a group of commonly controlled stations, Class A stations whose predicted Grade B contours are physically contiguous to each other may locate their main studio within any of these contours. If a Class A station is one of a group of commonly controlled Class A stations, but its predicted Grade B contour is not physically contiguous to that of another Class A station in the commonly owned group, its main studio shall be located within its own predicted Grade B contour. Alternatively, a Class A television station shall maintain a main studio at the site used by the station as of November 29, 1999...

Section 73.1125 of the FCC
Rules and Regulations: Station Main Studio Location

Simply Put:

"Location, location, location."

Real Estate Mantra of the 1990's

chapter three

move or stay? the site selection process

Many factors will influence your decision to renovate or relocate. Understanding these factors and weighing them against your specific circumstances will lead to your decision.

With the correct team assembled and a clear idea about space needs, the next step is to consider and compare a variety of location options. Clearly, engineering limitations will play a factor when first considering various sites as will a broad variety of other issues. These include ease of access for the staff, safety, station vehicle storage, and parking to name a few.

One big question – Cost?

When comparing sites, we strongly encourage looking at both initial and long-term costs. Often the site that seems like a great lease deal will cost more to build or operate or have "hidden" costs such as parking. Comparing the costs of building at various locations is, of course, part of the process. Looking at the costs associated with various sites over a ten-year period is probably a much more realistic comparison.

Ultimately the goal of any project is to create a fully functional place that operates well within the community at large. The chapter will help develop the criteria needed for the decision-making process.

Stay

The scale of needed renovations may be the largest influence in whether to stay in your existing facility. To remain, the following factors should be considered:

Growth

How has the size of various departments changed? If the overall scale of your facility does not need to grow but, internally, various departments have grown or scaled back, it may be most sensible to simply redefine the floor plan of your space.

Own vs. Lease

If you own your building and it will last for another 20-30 years, renovating may be the fastest, most affordable solution. In addition, if you are in a lease situation and have the flexibility to change spaces, grow within the building, add equipment, etc. the cost savings of not having to build new facility may outweigh the reasons for relocating. The lease may also be significantly cheaper than it would be in a new location.

The Neighborhood and Community

Is the current facility a physical icon in the community? Understanding the role in your surrounding neighborhood may show that moving could have an adverse impact on your listening base and promotional efforts. Also, for the same reasons addressed under moving, maybe the area has changed in a way that benefits your current situation.

Technology

Have you recently upgraded your infrastructure? Are the needed improvements minor enough to make for a simple fix?

Impact on Staff

Emotional connection and staff disruption are very significant factors in your current facility. Relocating away from where many of the staff live may affect the work environment and productivity of the employees.

Move

Making the decision to move your facility is based on a variety of factors. Depending on your needs, one or all of the following considerations could impact the decision.

Growth

Have you outgrown your facility or have your needs changed? Changes in format, management, sales, the consolidation (combining multiple locations or departments under one roof), corporate spin-offs, change in station number–any of these or other reasons could lead to your decision to move.

Own vs. Lease

If you own the building and the infrastructure is tired, it may be cost-effective to sell and relocate. Leasing a space may inhibit your ability to effectively renovate or take over more space, essentially requiring you to find a more suitable location.

The Neighborhood and Community

It is not uncommon for radio stations to be located in areas that, over time, have deteriorated, have become too expensive, or have had major zoning changes.

Technology

The cost of retrofitting your current space in order to have the most up-to-date and advanced wiring, sound, and production capabilities has the possibility of making the decision for you. Understanding your current situation and future needs will assist in knowing the more cost effective approach to your construction needs.

Impact on Staff

Relocating to ar away from an area where a majority of your staff resides can have a great impact on work. Also, taking into considerations local infrastructure availability is helpful–where will the staff eat lunch? How close is the post office? Do staff members have to drive far off site everyday. Is lunch a short walk or drive down the street?

Scenario: Stay, Expand, Renovate

Cox Radio – Orlando, Florida

Given the significant attributes of this location, the decision to stay was a common goal. The challenge was a realizable solution. This case study presents several planning points when evaluating move/stay options.

In this example, the owner possessed enough property to accommodate a significant addition. However, the combination of new space requirements, additional parking, and locally imposed storm water management demands exceeded the immediate available buildable area.

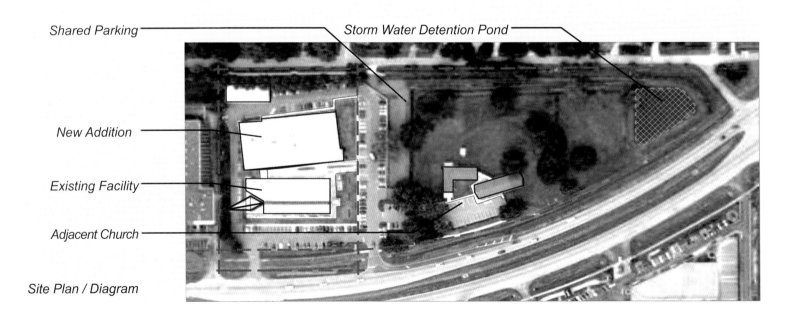

Shared Parking

Storm Water Detention Pond

New Addition

Existing Facility

Adjacent Church

Site Plan / Diagram

Initial feasibility studies explored multiple story schemes that reduced the overall foot print while accommodating new site requisites. These schemes were declined as the multi-story facility imposed unacceptable disruptions to operations and the station's general work flow.

After careful planning, diligent meetings, and thoughtful negotiations, an agreement was made with the station's neighboring church. Initial site improvements were made to the church's property on behalf of the station in exchange for the ability to use portions of the property for storm water management and some occasional overflow parking.

In so doing, both the church's objectives were fulfilled and a cost-effective, single-story structure was realized for the facility. Key throughout the process was the development of mutual benefits that were above and beyond individual objectives. While this example is unique, it does highlight the value of being a good neighbor and mindful of the community at large.

Building Entry

Scenario: Stay, Expand and Renovate

Cox Radio – Greenville, South Carolina

After an exhaustive search for affordable alternatives–both in and out of the Greenville business district–space adjacent to Cox Radio's existing facility on the fourth floor of a downtown office building became available.

As a result of consolidation, the existing studios and tech center had been cobbled together. It was generally agreed upon that there was little of value worth saving. Long deferred maintenance of offices and support spaces along with a new lease further justified a rethinking of the existing conditions and facility operations.

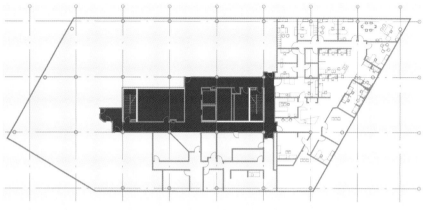

Existing Plan

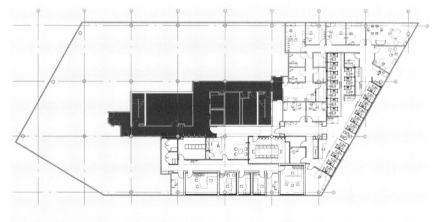

Expanded and Renovated Plan

New Air Studio

After developing a space-use program and confirming both wants and needs, it was agreed that funds could be best allocated by simply updating–paint, carpet, furniture, etc.– some areas. Management and accounting offices and some support spaces such as storage and the kitchen remained intact while the rest of the floor was demolished This required phasing and short-term use of other space in the building.

Practically, it made sense that the first pieces built were the studios, technical support areas and new lobby and that they were placed in the expansion space. With appropriate dust barriers in place and some doubling up of offices, this part of the project was completed with minor inconvenience to the staff. With this piece of infrastructure in place, the remaining spaces could be renovated in two phases allowing for minimal disruption.

Support Space

Scenario: Move, Buy, and Renovate

Entercom Communications – Kansas City, Kansas

With this example, the decision to move represents innocence lost. For years, the station enjoyed prominent community recognition. However the actual broadcast originated from a lone tower nested in a corn field at the edge of town.

Over the course of time, the station grew at the tower site, the corn fields were replaced by furrows of development, and a new set of neighbors and interests blossomed. After exhaustive studies, no effective addition to the existing station could resolve local zoning requirements, prompting the decision to move.

Initial efforts inscribed general locations that considered accessibility, desirable attributes, and station visibility. These were then cross-referenced with broadcast uplink and line-of-sight requirements.

The resulting map identified feasible locations and the basis for initial property search with the real estate broker. Through the process of elimination, several candidates were established for assessment and initial test fit and feasibility planning.

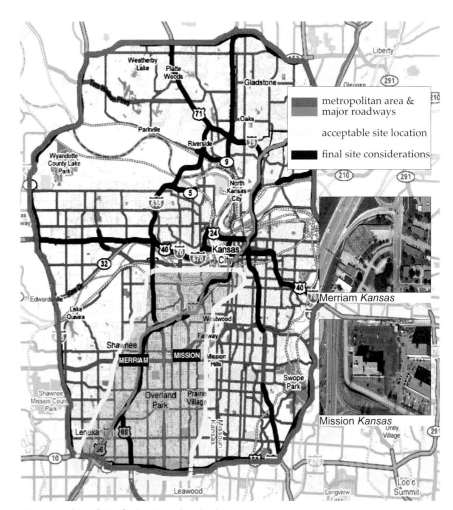

Kansas City Site Selection Analysis

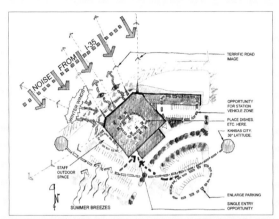

Merriam *Kansas*

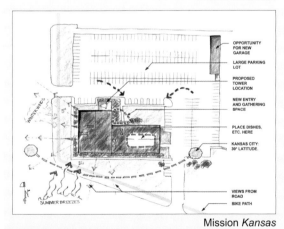

Mission *Kansas*

Site Studies

In the end, Entercom negotiated for and bought a 60,000-sq.-ft. facility, although the programmatic needs called for 40,000 square feet. The remaining space was to be leased and provide additional income. It will also present opportunities for future expansion.

Main Lobby

Site Selection

Typically, criteria determining the location of the station require the input and experience of several professionals. As discussed in Chapter One, this is organized around the management team and typically includes the broadcast engineer, a real estate broker, and the architect with their set of core consultants.

Refer back to the team you assembled in Chapter One. Many will play an important role in assessing your options in selecting a site whether you are staying or moving.

In most leasing situations, the broker's fees are paid for by the landlord upon completion of the lease. Similarly, if a building is being acquired, commissions are paid by the seller to the real estate office. While the real estate broker is on board to represent you in this transaction, there is an inherent conflict of interest if they are being paid on a percentage basis. While usually not an issue, to assure an unbiased representation, another option is to hire the broker as a consultant on an hourly or project basis.

Clearly, the Director of Engineering is an integral and critical part of the entire project process, and site selection is no exception. Their role early on will be to determine which sites are permissible legally and technically feasible.

Accessibility

The station's architect, in charge of planning and design, will advise how the facility must satisfy and adhere to both local and national laws and statutes dealing with access for the disabled. These are described in the Americans With Disabilities Act (ADA) which covers such elements as access ramps, toilet stall doors, etc.

"Accessibility" also involves movement of equipment, relationship to major thoroughfares, service by public transportation, etc.

Department Access

Certain departments require easy in-and-out access. Usually, the engineering staff and/or promotions personnel need to transport equipment for remote broadcasts. Site selection should be addressed with consideration to these needs early on.

Parking Access

A station with a strong interview or performance component may want to consider the ease of access, from streets and highways, to designated parking areas, and on into the correct studio within the building. Sufficient parking for both staff and station vehicles is always a concern.

Transportation Access

In many urban areas, public transportation is a consideration in site selection. Parking is a primary issue that will impact choice. A downtown location may be unsuitable because providing sufficient parking makes the site more expensive on an operating basis when averaged out on a 10-year projection. On the other hand, being at the center of activity may easily justify these costs.

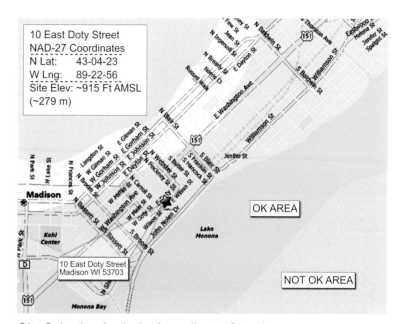

10 East Doty Street
NAD-27 Coordinates
N Lat: 43-04-23
W Lng: 89-22-56
Site Elev: ~915 Ft AMSL
(~279 m)

10 East Doty Street
Madison WI 53703

OK AREA

NOT OK AREA

Site Selection Analysis: According to Signal
Entercom Communications
Madison

Road Access

Sales personnel want to be close to major roadways for ease and convenience. When a station hosts an event for its advertisers, turnout will be higher if the station is auto friendly.

Design Criteria For Site Selection

Just as all radio is local, each design and the process of evaluating sites require a unique review. Accordingly, there is not one formula when in pursuit of the selection of a new facility site. However, when looking at the industry as a whole, there are elements that are common to most, if not all, broadcast buildings.

Engineering

A direct line of sight to the transmitter is one of the primary requisites. Securing this link can improve quality and reduce costs–both initial and recurring.

This analysis should also take into account:

- Ease of roof access for equipment maintenance and upgrades.
- Adequate and affordable cooling.
- Ample and "clean" power.
- Limited RF conflicts.
- The ability to build a tower (if required.) -See NIMBY discussion on page 60.
- Easy in-and-out site access for remote vehicles and required equipment.

Preliminary Site Possibility Sketch
Entercom Communications
Kansas City

Station Addition
Clear Channel Communications
Tulsa

Visibility

Selecting a site for new construction or expansion is a combination of what is needed, what management wants, and what the station will be allowed to do.

A majority of urban and suburban facilities are in multi-tenant office buildings. A prime advantage here is that by leasing the space, the station does not have the responsibility of maintaining the building. That being said, if the station opts to own the building, it has full control of its own space and exterior image.

Additionally, such considerations as real estate tax advantages and appreciation in the value of the property have to be weighed against the cost of leasing a comparable amount of space. In most situations, local codes will determine the size and type of external signage, height, acceptable materials, electronic components, etc.

Internal Super Graphic Along Atrium Glazing
Chancellor Media
Minneapolis

Achieving Visibility

The value of visibility can be achieved in many ways. The three massing studies shown to the right were for a group of stations along a busy road. While local codes restricted large signage, the building itself became the "sign" of the facility.

Similarly, the large sign in one of the main halls of Cities 97 in Minneapolis (opposite) is visible from the atrium lobby of the building. It is both integral to the design of the facility and a big part of the public image.

Massing Studies
Cox Radio
Babylon

Expansion Opportunities

An organization has been described as a living organism. As such, it will be altered and modified during its lifetime. Changes of a broadcasting company's group, cluster size, or its management structure may take place. If so, the station itself may need to expand or contract the physical space it occupies in the future. This possibility should be kept in mind during the search process.

Flexibility

Many types of spaces can be adaptively reused to serve as a broadcast facility. The architect will prepare an analysis for a potential renovation, or a comparison of several renovation candidates. Station management can study the proposals to develop projections based on three, five, and seven-year estimates. They can then evaluate estimated costs and use options.

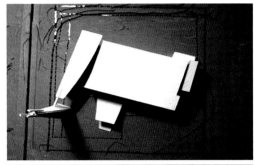

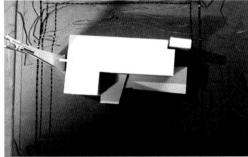

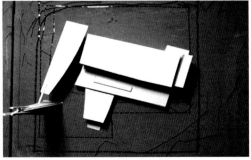

Massing Models
KPLU at Pacific Lutheran University
Tacoma

Searching for the Suitable Location

NIMBY: The Not-In-My-Backyard syndrome.
Don't be surprised if the community spreads the Un–Welcome mat. Residents and possibly local businesses may be concerned about increased traffic, noise and dirt from construction vehicles, potential disruption of living or operating patterns, and any number of real or imagined situations that can thwart a station's building program. If combined with other limitations such as zoning and electrical power requirements, site selection narrows quickly.

Conversely, the station can be courted and even offered incentives by neighborhoods, municipalities, or states. They consider the station's presence as a public asset and would take pride that its address is in their locale. Consider the tower as an opportunity, rather than a problem. For example, when building their new facility in Kansas City, Entercom considered illuminating their new tower according to the calendar events and sports team themes. For example, blue when the Kansas City Royals baseball team is in town, and pink for Breast Cancer Awareness Month.

Construction
Cox Radio
Orlando

The Neighborhood

A radio station is a commercial enterprise and as such may undergo considerable scrutiny wherever its building will be located: urban, suburban, ex-urban, or rural. Zoning regulations are a form of scrutiny; community evaluation is another. The architect and often station management will be called upon to present the purpose and details of the proposed headquarters.

Some executive boards and community groups will welcome the station to the neighborhood. Others will be strongly opposed. Broadcasters and their design consultants should be prepared to make their case in a clear, friendly manner.

Broadcast Facilities-for reasons such as format, editorial policies, or its on-air personalities (or guests) are occasionally the target of destructive and criminal activities. Ultimately, this will impact community response, the facility's design, and the selection of materials.

At this point, the designer and station management should investigate the pros and cons of renting space in an existing building versus construction of their own structure.

A recommended technique, to assist in the comparison, is the preparation of an analysis which examines a 10-year cycle of the options under consideration:

- construction costs
- energy expenses
- other utilities
- taxes
- maintenance

Often a preliminary meeting with community leaders in an "informal setting" is a time- and cost-effective way of assuring approvals.

Tower Study
Entercom Communications
Kansas City

Operational Considerations

Is it realistic to operate the station while renovating and/or expanding the existing facility? Yes, but there are some major concerns.

Construction Protection

Construction debris and drywall dust are anathema to broadcast equipment and torture to people with allergies. The architect and the contractor will specify protective techniques that will minimize debris and dust transmittal to occupied areas.

Location During Construction

Staff members like to maintain their work pattern in a place in which they are familiar. If possible, provisions should be taken for this. Anticipate lower productivity when arranging for temporary quarters. However, downtime is reduced and productivity can be maintained by keeping personnel in their original location, and excited by the project. If the station is associated with the community's growth, listeners like to maintain a continuity of visual recognition with the station. This can be an asset.

Potential Cost Savings

There are potential cost savings associated with renovation including moving costs and negotiating reduced construction charges. In a renovation, there may be areas that need only cosmetic upgrading, a less expensive undertaking than constructing a new facility.

Construction
Cox Radio
Orlando

Design and Photo Credits

Getting Started Check List

— What is the current facility situation that is causing the decision to consider renovation, expansion, or relocation?

— What do staff and visitors like and/or dislike about the existing facility(ies)?

— Identify and map 15-20 major clients, advertisers, etc.
  Where are they located?
  Should you be in that area?

— Are there any unusual parking or storage needs?

— Where do most staff live (track through zip codes) and how are they most likely to get to work?

— Are there any special security needs?

— Are there any special requirements with regards to guests or deliveries?

Site Selection Check List

— Will zoning allow the needs of your facility?

— Is it a suitable location for future expansion?

— What is the proximity to staff residences?

— Does it have easy access to major roads?

— What is the proximity to supporting facilities and companies (copy center, lunch shops, promotions agency, etc.)?

— What are the technological impacts? - Is it an easy move for engineering?

View of Lobby from Main Hall
Cox Radio
Jacksonville

chapter four

assembling the facility's components

The well-crafted facility is built to support the long-term and short-term goals of the broadcaster. The task of the architect and other design team members is to fully understand those goals and create a physical manifestation of those ideas.

This chapter investigates the proven patterns that have evolved and the process of how the assembly of rooms can further support big ideas. The organization of key components is what fundamentally differentiates facilities and is integral to the day-to-day culture.

By and large, all broadcast facilities share the same basic kit of parts. Large market or small, almost all have sales and marketing components, space devoted to management, and areas designed to facilitate programming and production. They all need the technological means to get the signal out to the public.

And, whether the station(s) is located on the fifty-third floor of a major office building or in a freestanding structure on an independent site, it is the assembly of those rooms and departments that ultimately determines how the facility will function and present itself to the world beyond its walls.

Pieces of the Puzzle

While studios and their associated support spaces and offices are usually a construction class unto themselves requiring specialized walls and windows, it is their location within the facility and their spatial relationship to the other working departments that will have the biggest impact on the sense of community in any broadcast structure.

Air Studio Corridor
CBS Radio
Pittsburgh

Production and Programming

Most radio stations or station clusters include some or all of the following components in the production and programming areas. While there are many exceptions to the rule, typically it makes sense to cluster them in one area.

- on-air or main studios
- control studios
- production studios
- news studios
- tracking or small dubbing studios
- newsroom and associated support spaces
- green room or on-air guest waiting space
- specialty show offices.
- programming, music, news director office(s) or workspace(s)
- music
- call-in support space(s)
- kitchen or small coffee bar if not near the one serving the entire staff
- toilet room(s) if not near those serving the rest of the facility
- Occasionally, the traffic and continuity people are located in or with direct access to the production/programming area(s).

Engineering/Technical Support Areas
While few new facilities have more than
one TOC (aka Technical Operations Center
or Rack Room), it is not uncommon to have
small support rooms throughout the facility,
typically located to reduce wiring runs or needs.
These spaces are composed of the following
components.

- equipment racks for broadcast, IT, and
  telephone equipment
- punch blocks and cross-connects for
  wiring integration
- dedicated or discretely controlled HVAC
  system

While it is advantageous to have the TOC
centrally located to the studios, it should also
be in close proximity to the tower and satellite
dishes for studio transmitter links.

Another factor in TOC location is its immediacy
to an electrical service room which contains
back-up power transfers switch, UPS, and other
related electrical equipment. The TOC also needs
to be secured and carefully monitored.

Lobby Area
Cox Radio
Jacksonville

Promotions

It is not uncommon for the promotions professionals and their support space to be in a number of locations throughout the facility. Depending on variables such as real estate costs, building configuration, and format, it may, for example, make sense to locate the bulk of the department near sales or programming. Storage areas and intern work-up spaces can be located near exits, or even off-site. The prize closet is usually the responsibility of the Promotions Department and located near the receptionist. Yet rarely is the entire department located in or adjacent to the highly visible public lobby.

While format will impact space use needs –whether broken up throughout the facility or consolidated into one area–most promotions departments will include parts or all of the following areas:

- promotions director(s)
- marketing director
- promotions staff
- prize closet
- small, medium and large scale storage

If the format warrants, consider a special promotions closet for staff and interns that has limited access to the overall facility. This secured space can be stocked in advance for those who need to pick up materials, assignments, station vehicles, etc., -without giving full access.

Promotions Van
Clear Channel Communications
Indianapolis

- intern work area(s)
- promotions preparations
- vehicle storage area

Sales

As discussed in Chapter Two, the Sales Department can absorb as much as twenty percent of the space needs in a commercial radio facility. Even if educational or non-profit stations have a smaller percentage devoted to marketing and sales, this component of any facility demands a significant piece of real estate.

Since there are several components shared by all sales and marketing people, sales has a history of being massed in one area although there are several successful cases of decentralization. Most radio facilities have much of the sales staff in an open office environment with some enclosed offices for management and private meeting areas. Most also include some or all of the following:

- director of sales
- general and/or local sales manager(s)
- sales assistant
- sales associates

Sales Area
CBS Radio
Baltimore

- sales work-up area
- sales conference room or meeting space

Management Offices

It is not uncommon for the General Manger's senior staff to be situated nearby. The immediate access and the ability to discuss strategies without making a trip to another section of the facility does have some advantages. (The counterpoint to that approach is to put the senior level people within their departmental areas: Director of Sales in the Sales Department, the Director of Marketing near Promotions or Sales, etc.). Organizational schemes that include a consolidated management or business area might include:

- general manager
- GM assistant
- human resources
- accounting/business manager
- program director
- director of sales
- operations manager
- traffic manager

- director of marketing
- director of engineering

Business Offices

The controller and the financial staff (along with the Traffic Department) are perhaps the employees most likely to be in their offices on a day-to-day basis—often justifying access to windows. Characteristically, they tend to be located off the beaten track affording them quiet, confidential, and secure space.

Traffic

The Traffic Department, by convention, has been situated near the sales staff as that is the traditional route for booking air time. It is, not uncommon for the traffic staff to share an area with or report to accounting, or even associate closely with the programming staff. The lesson is that these people need to be easily accessed by many members of the staff yet be in easily secured spaces.

Support Spaces

Essentially, these necessary areas are shared by

Consider the idea of building "phone booths." Often, the need to make private phone calls results in conference rooms being used by one sales associate. An almost closet-sized room with a telephone and computer access can afford some privacy and generally reduce the noise level in the sales area.

Also consider small meeting areas distributed throughout the facility. This is often achieved simply by widening a corridor.

Meeting Area
Cox Radio
Honolulu

Assembling the Pieces

There are three basic methods to organize a radio station facility. While individual program needs and context will cause adjustments to these basic forms, in the end, all well-designed facilities fall into one of these categories:

- Departments Around a Core
- Independent Living
- The Campus Plan

Reception
Chancellor Media
Cincinnati

Reception
CBS Radio
Baltimore

Departments Around a Core

In this type of facility, the goal is to create one major space with a series of portals into all of the various departments. All or most of the studios and programming are in one area, all of sales in another, etc. Often, the various support spaces such as kitchen(s), conference rooms, copy/mail rooms, etc. are also associated with this central core.

All departments are, by and large, combined so that production, programming, sales, etc. all enter directly from the central space or core, offering direct access to shared conference, copying, lunch, and management areas.

This form generates a simple plan that encourages interaction between various departments, as everyone has to pass through this common space on a regular basis. Done correctly, it is also an efficient solution. Many hallways can be combined into one major space affording opportunities for small gatherings and one-on-one informal meetings without having to use a conference room.

The example of Chancellor Media in Cincinnati, successfully used the notion of creating central space that largely eliminated dark and narrow hallways.

Core Plan Diagram
Bloomfield & Associates, Architects

Case Study – Chancellor Media, Cincinnati

Project Background:

Designed shortly after deregulation in the mid-90's, Chancellor Media sought to assemble their Cincinnati holdings under one roof. They selected a floor of a new multi-story office building to build this first-of-its-kind facility.

Design Analysis:

The business model called for one sales group, one central production facility, one programming department, one management/accounting support core, etc. The "core" in this case is a combination lobby and main hall that connects all of these separate areas. The result is a facility where all members of the staff must go through the lobby whenever leaving their departmental area and interact on a regular basis.

Key

■ Administrative
■ Sales/Development
▒ Engineering
■ Studios/Prod.
▓ Promotions
▒ Support
☐ Common / Unused

Floor Plan

Independent Living

This assembling of pieces is referred to as a "tribal approach." Stations are clustered or grouped as opposed to assembling like activities, as in the "Departments Around a Core" type we just discussed.

In the first example shown here, the Sandusky group of stations in Seattle chose to create three clusters or "pods" for their five stations. Each holds programming, production, sales, traffic, and promotions for the individual station. They come together along a spine that also holds remaining components that make sense to share: engineering, conference rooms, kitchen, reception, and storage/mail room.

The advantage is that it encourages competition and independence between stations. It also mitigates or relieves the kind of problems often seen when competing formats and their associated cultures are brought under one roof.

Tribal Plan Diagram
Bloomfield & Associates, Architects

Case Study – Sandusky Radio, Seattle

Project Background:

With several very distinct formats and a long history of competing for similar market share, it made sense to think of creating an environment that allows for individual station groups to coexist within one supportive facility

Design Analysis:

If the initial goal was to create a competitive environment between stations, the solution lay in designing a supportive environment for all concerned. The individual "pods" that contain studios, sales space, traffic, promotions, etc. for the individual stations have the benefit of sharing conference rooms, kitchen, engineering and reception in a large common lobby. The effect is that each station is able to benefit from the use of these shared components yet remain fiercely individual.

Key
▩ Administrative
▩ Sales/Development
▩ Engineering
▩ Studios/Prod.
▩ Promotions
▩ Support
☐ Common / Unused

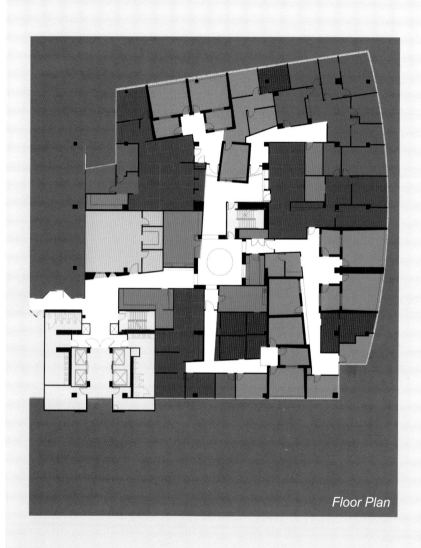

Floor Plan

The Campus Plan

Traditional campus planning is based on placing significant elements of the college (chapel, library, main academic building, etc.) on opposite ends of the site and then filling in the spaces between with academic or residential buildings. Similarly, this concept of organizing the facility can be applied to a group of stations. Here major elements are separated and then connected with the support facilities typically included in a group of stations.

Characteristically, this method of organization works best for a group of four of more stations. Components such as management or programming and production areas can be easily set up an independent group.

Campus Plan Diagram
Bloomfield & Associates, Architects

Case Study – CBS Radio, Baltimore

Project Background:

This CBS facility was built in an existing single-story office building. All five stations have a long history of local programming and production. Sales and Promotions compete for similar market share. Accounting, Traffic, and Engineering are centralized.

Design Analysis:

The main Air studios are clustered on either end of the facility creating "Anchors". This allows for some shared areas such as a Green Room. Sales and Programming-including dubbing and production studios-to be clustered according to individual station, giving each their own distinctive entry.

Other shared "support"-kitchen, toilets, lobby, engineering, management, traffic etc. Are located on the other side of the "Campus Quad." The result is an efficient, well-organized facility which offers individual station identity and flexibility.

Key
■ Administrative
■ Sales/Development
▦ Engineering
▦ Studios/Prod.
▦ Promotions
▦ Support
□ Common / Unused

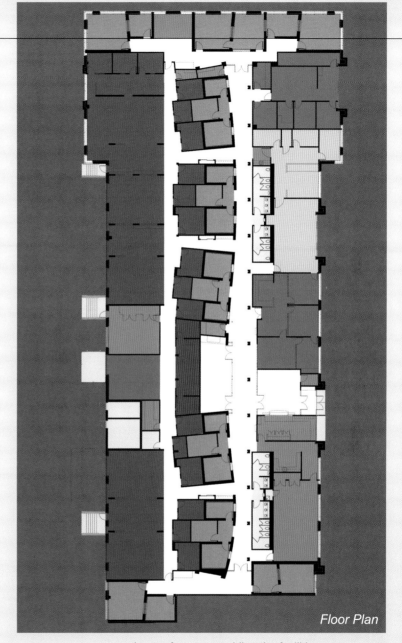

Floor Plan

Design and Photo Credits

Understanding Your Departmental Relationships

The following is a list of questions that may help determine how various departments and their interrelationship might be structured:

— Should department heads (Directors of Programming, Engineering, Accounting, etc. be centrally located with the General Manager or dispersed within the facility?

— Are there historically any departments that work closely together that might not do so in other markets?

— Are there any departments that require a special need for access during off hours? Examples of this might be a format that has the Promotions Department working weekends or one with significant remote equipment requirements.

— How much cross-selling is there between stations? Should that take a physical form in the layout of sales areas?

— Is the promotions staff one department or should they be distributed according to sales or programming staff?

— Should the new facility be organized to encourage competition between stations or seen as one large team?

— Should support spaces such as conference rooms, coffee/kitchen areas, toilets, storage, etc. be centralized, or distributed throughout the facility?

Lobby
Cox Radio
Greenville

chapter five

establishing a budget and sticking to it

The principle objective of a project budget is to form and confirm consensus of expectations and of priorities. This section will describe the basic principles, components, and management strategies of a project budget and how priorities, relationships, and responsibilities can be established to insure a successful project.

With any undertaking as complex as a broadcast facility, a diverse set of personalities and requisites will converge over the course of time.

From initial planning, through construction, and years after the facility is occupied, the project budget documents a set of informed decisions and agreement between diverse interests.

This section will also describe, budgetary issues raised elsewhere in this edition. It will introduce alternative strategies that can trim costs and time without sacrificing quality, and allow you to stick to your budget.

Priorities, Principles, and Objectives: Correlating Time, Quality, and Cost

When faced with the task of establishing a project budget, each budgetary item creates a relationship between time, cost, and quality.

An extreme example is where time is ultra critical and you must be out of your space due to lease expirations or an emergency such as a fire. In order to meet the schedule of these rare examples, the quality will most likely diminish and your new space will come at a higher price.

It is the responsibility of the project leaders to strategically set the tone and establish the relationships between time, quality, and cost to form project goals. While the purpose of a project budget may be perceived as a necessity to fulfill an immediate need…"What does it cost?"… the project's budget is far-reaching.

Designated personnel with input from supporting staff and design team members should carefully consider issues of expansion, adaptability, and cost of operations. To incorporate this, the project budget's time frame should be expanded to a 10 to 15-year period. When considered in this light, the true budgetary goals can be confirmed.

In response to an ever-competitive market, there is the desire to reduce time and costs while maintaining quality. While there is no

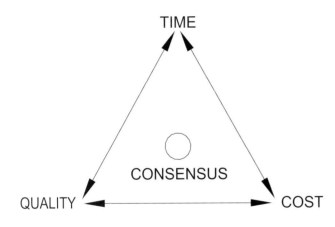

Budget Diagram
Bloomfield & Associates, Architects

silver bullet to resolve this inherent conflict, the diligent maintenance of the project budget can diminish the impact of surprises.

To be effective, the Project Budget should be considered a working document that is updated and adjusted with more accurate information throughout the course of a project.

After initial scopes of work are defined and associated costs established, each line item should be carefully reviewed for comprehensiveness and necessity. When all line items are checked and looked at as a whole, the priorities and budgetary goals will have to be adjusted to assure overall conformity. This process of asking and answering will continue until procurement is made.

Central Core
Cox Radio
Birmingham

The Project Budget

One of the keys to a successful project is identifying all of the required items. This sounds simple but more often than not, items that upset a budget are ones never accounted for from the outset. Organization of the numerous budgetary items is another key. There are several useful terms that you will encounter. These are:

- **Up-Front Costs**
- **Carrying Costs**
- **Soft Costs**
- **Hard Costs**

While there will be little consensus on the exact definitions within the industry, these categories serve as helpful touchstones to outline a budget.

Up-Front Costs are expenses incurred during the land/lease negotiation phase. **Carrying Costs** are expenses incurred between land / lease negotiations and occupancy of the building. **Soft Costs** are expenses incurred for professionals involved in the project, **Hard Costs** are expenses that typically include construction, furnishings, and equipment.

When initiating the budgeting process, invariably personalities will place different items into different categories. For the most part it doesn't matter where they go as long as they are accounted for and everyone knows where they are. The project budget worksheet depicted on pages 89-90 represents basic categories for two common scenarios: a new facility from the ground up, and a tenant fit out.

Owner-Provided Items

The unique aspect of a project budget for your facility is the Broadcast Engineering category. This sub-category typically includes systems and equipment associated with the actual broadcast. The station usually purchases these items directly, and the scope is facility-specific. These have come to form a unique category known as "Owner-Provided Items."

By and large, the responsibility for defining this budgetary category falls on the shoulders of the station's Director of Engineering. This can represent 20 to 35 percent of the total project budget. It is very important that this item be carefully defined, and specified early on as equipment selection will impact the design criteria for consultants such as the HVAC and electrical engineers.

Contingency Allowances

Contingency allowances serve several purposes throughout the budgeting process. In the early stages they act as placeholders to cover associated costs for items that have not been defined. During the procurement and construction phases, they serve as placeholders to account for escalation, unforeseen conditions, and oversights. While oversights are not desirable, and to the greatest degree possible can be reduced through careful planning, they do occur. Contingency allowances are a useful tool to ease the impact of the discoveries.

The contingency allowances are adjusted as the process advances. In the early stages of a project budget, contingency allowances are normally held in the range of 10 to 15 percent for each category. As the project advances and discrete aspects are defined, the percentages can be dropped to 7 to 10 percent.

Once procurement has been established, the construction contingency typically can be dropped again to 3 to 5 percent.

Air Studio
Entercom Communications
Greenville

Up Front Costs

New Facility	Tenant Fit Out	No.	ACCT. Name	Initial	Updated 00.00.00
		1000	**Feasibility Planning**		
X	X		Due Diligence Assessment	$0.00	$0.00
X	X		Feasibility Study	$0.00	$0.00
X	X		Zoning Review & Approval	$0.00	$0.00
X	X		Legal Review	$0.00	$0.00
X			Land Purchase	$0.00	$0.00
X	X		(Incentives)	$0.00	$0.00
			Contingency 10%	$0.00	$0.00
			Division Subtotal	**$0.00**	**$0.00**

Carrying Costs

New Facility	Tenant Fit Out	No.	ACCT. Name	Initial	Updated 00.00.00
		2000	**New Site / Location**		
X			Debt Service	$0.00	$0.00
	X		Rent	$0.00	$0.00
X			Real Estate Taxes	$0.00	$0.00
X	X		Utilities	$0.00	$0.00
X			Insurance	$0.00	$0.00
X	X		Maintenance	$0.00	$0.00
			subtotal	$0.00	$0.00
		2500	**Current Site / Location**		
X			Debt Service	$0.00	$0.00
	X		Rent	$0.00	$0.00
X			Real Estate Taxes	$0.00	$0.00
X	X		Utilities	$0.00	$0.00
X			Insurance	$0.00	$0.00
X	X		Maintenance	$0.00	$0.00
			subtotal	$0.00	$0.00
			Contingency 5%	$0.00	$0.00
			Division Subtotal	**$0.00**	**$0.00**

Project Budget Work Sheet
Bloomfield & Associates, Architects

Soft Costs

New Facility	Tenant Fit Out	No.	ACCT. Name	Initial	Updated 00.00.00
		3000	**Design Team**		
X	X		Architect	$0.00	$0.00
X			Civil Engineering	$0.00	$0.00
X			Geo Technical Engineering	$0.00	$0.00
X	?		Structural Engineering	$0.00	$0.00
X	X		MEP Engineering	$0.00	$0.00
X	X		Furniture Consultant	$0.00	$0.00
X	X		Acoustical Consultant	$0.00	$0.00
X	X		Lighting Consultant	$0.00	$0.00
X	X		Cost Estimator	$0.00	$0.00
X	X		Expense Reimbursable	$0.00	$0.00
			Contingency 3%	$0.00	$0.00
			Division Subtotal	**$0.00**	**$0.00**

Hard Costs

New Facility	Tenant Fit Out	No.	ACCT. Name	Initial	Updated 00.00.00
			General Contractor Construction		
X	X	4100	Hard Construction	$0.00	$0.00
	X	4200	(Tenant Improvement Allowance)	$0.00	$0.00
			Contingency 10%	$0.00	$0.00
			subtotal	$0.00	$0.00
			Owner Provided Technical Construction		
X	X	5000	Broadcast Engineering	$0.00	$0.00
X	X	5100	Office Computer System	$0.00	$0.00
X	X	5200	Security System	$0.00	$0.00
X	X	5300	Phone Intercom System	$0.00	$0.00
X	X	5400	Generator	$0.00	$0.00
		5500	Next	$0.00	$0.00
			Contingency 10%	$0.00	$0.00
			subtotal	$0.00	$0.00
			Owner Provided Items & Services		
X	X	6000	Furniture	$0.00	$0.00
X	X	6100	Office Equipment / Appliances	$0.00	$0.00
X	X	6200	Moving	$0.00	$0.00
X	X	6300	Storage	$0.00	$0.00
X	X	6400	Decommissioning Current Site	$0.00	$0.00
X	X	6500	Shipping	$0.00	$0.00
X	X	6600	Building Signage	$0.00	$0.00
		6700	Next	$0.00	$0.00
			Contingency 10%	$0.00	$0.00
			subtotal	$0.00	$0.00
			Division Subtotal	**$0.00**	**$0.00**
			Project total	**$0.00**	**$0.00**

Establishing Budgetary Values

Perhaps the best way to understand how monetary values are established for a project budget is to consider them in relation to project phases. The budget will undergo two principal defining moments, initially by the Feasibility Study and again during the design phase. The Project Budget Worksheet lists items you should anticipate. Designated team members and design professionals should verify the applicability of each before eliminating them from the Worksheet.

The Feasibility Study

The purpose of the Feasibility Study is to quickly present a snapshot of opportunities and constraints associated with each site. The goal is to identify the viable, weigh the tangibles, and select the optimal.

During this phase it is normal to compare several properties. Included in the comparisons are design options, due diligence analysis, and acquisition and improvement costs to establish project viability. The monetary values for **Up-Front Costs** and **Carrying Costs** incurred during the Feasibility Study are negotiated values for involved team members and typically carried as a lump sum.

Projected **Hard Costs** for the Feasibility Study are normally carried as dollars-per-square foot for required types of work. Design team members can assist in establishing these values. Costs for "Owner-Provided Items" are typically projected by the director of engineering and are usually based upon similar projects.

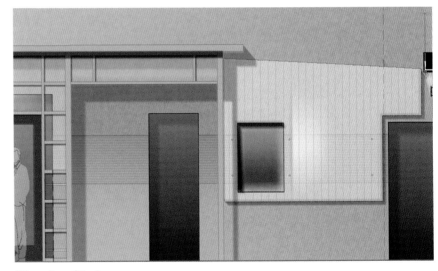

Elevation Study
CBS Radio
Baltimore

The Design Phase

Upon securing the property, establishing goals and accepting the project's viability, the project budget will undergo significant refinement throughout the design process. More accurate monetary values for **Hard Costs** will be established as specific *scopes of work* are defined for both general construction and broadcast integration.

Updated pricing can be secured through several sources. For general construction, an independent cost estimator can provide estimates as the scope of work develops. Another method is to secure estimating services directly through a General Contractor.

During the design phase, the Director of Engineering, in conjunction with their staff, can prepare detailed equipment and integration scopes of work which are used to secure pricing directly from vendors. During this phase it is appropriate to define the scope of "Owner-Provided Items" and begin coordination with design team members.

Keep in mind that pricing information is often time-dependant and exact costs will not be known until procurement has been made. To accommodate this inherent condition, every effort should be taken to secure pricing with time frames commensurate with the project's schedule. Given the dynamics of todays market this is becoming harder to do, and the contingency allowances can accommodate associated escalation expenses.

The chart below represents the disbursement of **Hard Costs** and **Soft Costs** for various sized facilities and should be used as a general guide for

	1 - 2 stations 4 - 7 studios 9,000 - 15,000 net sq ft	3 - 4 stations 8 - 13 studios 14,000 - 27,000 net sq ft	5 - 8 stations 15 - 24 studios 26,000 - 38,000 net sq ft
Construction	64%	54%	61%
Owner Provided Technical	20%	28%	23%
Furnishings and Office Equipment	6%	10%	7%
Professional Fees*	10%	8%	9%

* Note: This is a percentage of the project budget and not a percentage of construction.

Percentage of Project Budget
Bloomfield & Associates, Architects

Maintaining a Project Budget

Maintaining a Project Budget is simply that: *It is maintenance.* Like the maintenance of a car, your regular and diligent attention will yield a high-performing vehicle, getting you where you want to be. The maintenance of a Project Budget is no different. It is the regular confirmation and adjustment of priorities that will keep the budget on track during the feasibility and design phases.

Feasibility Study

During this phase, the maintenance of the project budget is predominantly task and deadline-driven. Specific tasks are delegated to responsible team members with clear delivery dates. Meetings are usually convened bi-weekly with the Project Budget updated accordingly.

Key to this phase is land/lease negotiations and acquisition strategy updates. Where applicable, the incentives packages and tax/depreciation planning options should be included in the review process. The Project Budget should also be adjusted to account for discoveries made during due diligence assessment, space utilization programming, and the design test fit to confirm project viability.

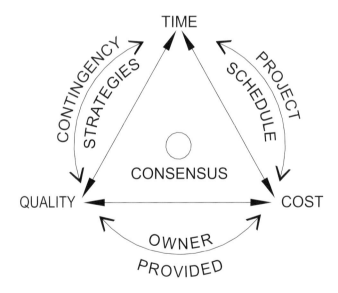

Budget Diagram
Bloomfield & Associates, Architects

Design Phase

At the onset of the design phase, additional pricing tools become available. The rigor of regular budget review meetings should be adhered to. One significant difference is that pricing for **Hard Costs** shifts from the general to the specific, as discrete scopes of work are designed and specified.

To facilitate revised pricing, it is prudent to set delivery date bench marks for design team member's documentation. It is acceptable practice during this phase to have 3-4 cost estimates prepared with the Project Budget updated accordingly.

Additionally, during this phase it is normal for **Up-Front Costs** and the **Carrying Costs** allotments to change very little. They are, however, open items and should be reviewed periodically to avoid surprises down the road.

Main Hall
CBS Radio
Baltimore

Sticking to the Project Budget

Throughout the course of a project, you will be confronted with tough choices, most of them without the benefit of 100 percent pricing, and almost all of them without the benefit of hind sight. This is the nature of the endeavor.

The project's budgetary success hinges upon leadership establishing goals and priorities that underpin the decision making-process while facilitating budget conformity. The blanketing statement, "You can't afford this," is perhaps not the best answer. A more productive approach would be to identify the priorities, why they are priorities, and have team members develop solutions that will achieve the goals.

There are several tools and management strategies that can facilitate budget conformity. The Project Budget itself is a working document. Utilization of its flow and structure is one way to stick to your budget.

Scope Reduction

Scope reduction modifications are one tool to stay on budget. The greatest financial benefit of this option is achieved when implemented during the planning and design phases and prior to commencement of final documentation. A common example is having two or three Heating, Ventilation and Air Conditioning (HVAC) systems outlined and priced.

While there may be significant cost benefits of one option over another, it is important that all involved understand the option's impact on the facility and your expectations. There will be discrete portions of a project where scope modifications studies should be implemented. Your design team can help identify them, keeping them on the screen so you can make an informed decision at the appropriate time.

Bid Alternates

Bid alternates are another tool at your disposal to assist in sticking to a budget. The bid alternate concept is simple: instead of doing this… what would it cost/save to do this? Descriptions for bid alternates are normally prepared by your design team and priced by the general contractor during the bidding and procurement period. To best utilize this option, there should be a significant difference in associated time and material costs for each bid alternate.

Contingency Strategies
What about "Plan B"?

Yes, you should have one (or more) of them. They should be identified, developed, and available for implementation during the corresponding project phase. "Plan B" options are essentially contingency plans developed to resolve issues when Plan A goes awry, without also absorbing adverse time and quality impacts.

Each project is unique and your contingency strategies should be developed to optimize Time, Quality, and Cost relationships, keeping in mind that as you optimize one of the three, the other two will lag.

- If the greatest minimal price is the priority, then control of the time frame may be sacrificed and the quality will most likely diminish.

- If you are on a tight budget and want a quality project, more time will be required to identify effective solutions. You should be prepared to spend more on your consultants for their time to research and develop less expensive solutions.

- Should time be of the essence and you absolutely have to vacate your facility, additional costs will be incurred to meet the deadline. You should expect additional hard costs associated with premium time during construction. Additional soft costs may be incurred to administer a multi-phased or fast-track project.

Admittedly, every project is unique and the permutations and impacts of contingency strategies are numerous. You will find, through discussions with team members, that the overall project tone will come to the surface.

Owner-Provided Items
Another tool to control costs are "Owner-Provided Items," and this continues to be an expanding category. These are items purchased directly by the station and not the General Contractor.

Within the industry, these items were usually limited to broadcast furnishings and equipment, but over time have expanded to include computers, IT, phone, security systems, and other discrete large ticket items. The advantage is that you attain quality at a reduced price. You get what you need and avoid delays, without the associated markup that a General Contractor would charge.

When "Owner-Provided Items" are identified early, your design team can facilitate project coordination. During construction, these items will at some point interface with those provided by the General Contractor.

To maximize the option's benefit, your design team can prepare directives with your staff to avoid overlaps and misses. The impact of these oversights can be significantly reduced with careful coordination between the Director of Engineering and the design team during the design and planning phases.

This method may require additional staff resources. Prior to considering or expanding the scope of this option, your Director of Engineering and support staff should confirm time availability for implementation.

Project Schedule

How the Project Schedule is structured is another tool to control costs. As a general rule, any measure that will reduce the overall project period will save money by reducing associated administrative costs.

If there is no "must-have" deadline, there may be financial benefits in letting the General Contractor establish the construction schedule to best deploy their resources. This appears contradictory, but projects are unique and your design team can assist in evaluating the options.

One way to reduce the overall construction time period and trim costs is to *pre-order long lead items*. This is particularly effective for large mechanical and electrical equipment. During the design phase, these items can be pre-specified to confirm performance and released for procurement.

Another schedule-related and avoidable source of surprise costs are delivery dates for early occupancy. The careful coordination and scheduling of studio and TOC turnover dates for integration and broadcast fit out can avoid land/lease extensions and associated moving costs.

When entering into a multi-phased project where partial occupancy is projected, the furniture and moving scope of work should be structured accordingly. The costs associated with multiple moves need to be accounted.

Given the diverse personalities and inherent human factors involved, the Project Schedule is an evolving document. When there are significant schedule modifications, the Project Budget should be reviewed and adjusted to address the impact of the changes.

Design and Photo Credits

p 82   Lobby
          Cox Radio
          Greenville, South Carolina
          Source: Bloomfield & Associates, Architects

p 85   Central Core
          Cox Radio
          Birmingham, Alabama
          Source: Bloomfield & Associates, Architects

p 87   Air Studio
          Entercom Communications
          Greenville, South Carolina
          Source: Bloomfield & Associates, Architects

p 90   Elevation Study
          CBS Radio
          Baltimore, Maryland
          Source: Bloomfield & Associates, Architects

p 93   Main Hall
          CBS Radio
          Baltimore, Maryland
          Source: Bloomfield & Associates, Architects

Project Budget Check List

– Establish budgetary goals

– Identify team members

– Delegate areas of responsibility

– Establish meeting schedule

– Establish deliverables and dates

– Identify contingency strategies

– Identify potential scope reductions

– Establish owner-provided items

– Establish and update budget values

– Establish and update contingency allowances

– Coordinate Budget with Project Schedule

"Those who ignore history are destined to repeat it."

George Santayana

chapter six

integration

Most of the heavy lifting in the planning and execution of these building projects falls to the General Manager and the Engineers. Both are integral in the design process, with managers typically taking the responsibility for budgets and overall concept, and the engineers assuming the lead for meeting schedules and specifications. This chapter focuses on the engineering side.

In preparing this book we were able to periodically interview some of the top working professionals in the industry today. The three included here provide a cross section of wisdom. They have broad experience at both the local and national level allowing for a vast resource of knowledge that will impact the outcome of most projects.

Charles Kinney **(CK)** is *Director of Engineering* for Cox Radio's holdings in Atlanta and regularly takes the lead in the design and construction of Cox projects nationally.

Mike Cooney **(MK)** is *Director of Engineering* for Entercom Communications Kansas City Market. He recently completed the construction of their new 40,000 SF facility.

Erich Steinnagel **(ES)** as *Regional Director of Engineering* for CBS Radio is responsible for both the five stations in his home market of Baltimore and for five other large markets nationwide.

When Designing Towers What Are Your Primary Considerations?

Location and Approvals:

CK: Look for a site allowable by the FCC: a tower as described for your station's license. Zoning is the primary issue. The tower should be located in a non-urbanized area but close enough to serve that region. With the wide-spread use of cellular phone service, people see more tower-mounted equipment. This has made them more sensitive to communication towers located in their areas.

MC: Allow adequate time for zoning and approvals. Where possible, the tower should be sized to accommodate more antennas than needed. In most cities, tower construction costs are significantly less than the amount of revenue that can be generated by leasing a portion of the tower. The accompanying electrical rooms and service should be part of the planning and design process. Soil conditions should also be confirmed as they will impact foundation type, size, and costs.

AM and FM Towers:

CK: The fundamental difference between an FM tower and an AM tower is that the antenna is a device mounted on the FM tower, while for AM the tower is the antenna. With the AM tower there is an additional component: the grounding system that radiates out from the tower's base in all directions. Radials extend horizontally the same distance that the tower is tall. The AM tower is essentially a resonate structure whose frequency is efficiently tuned by the tower's height, by the ground wave during the day, and the sky at night. Ground conductivity is also another consideration for the AM tower and is usually confirmed by a geotechnical consultant. The higher the soil's metal content the more conductive it is, and the better the signal will radiate. When the soil does not conduct effectively, chemical grounding rods can be inserted into the soil to increase conductivity.

Tower Grounding:

CK: Tower grounding in general is a critical issue. The transmission equipment and equipment racks should be bonded to each other and out to the tower. The last thing you want is one piece of equipment at one ground potential and another piece of equipment at a different ground potential. If this happens, it is likely that one piece of equipment will be blown up more than the other.

MC: Tower grounding is one of the most critical aspects and a qualified and experienced consultant should design the system. This measure can preserve existing equipment, avoid equipment replacement costs, and avoid down time.

Entrance Stair

Entercom Communications
Kansas City

What Are the Design Options and Considerations for Studio Transmitter Links?

Wireless vs. Direct:

CK: The first decision is whether you want a wireless link or a direct link through the phone company. There are advantages and disadvantages to both. The *advantage* of using the phone company is that you do not have to worry about fade problems from atmospheric conditions. With a T1 connection, you can easily have a bi-directional link to send your audio feeds out to the transmitter and receive satellite feeds and remote control data back. The *downside* is that you are committed to a utility and paying for recurring costs.

ES: We prefer to be independent from any utility or phone company. We also select *licensed microwave paths* because they are protected. Because we need improved connectivity for data to these sites, our options are running out and in some instances, we had to move to an unlicensed data path. We are working our way through that process and finding out how to extend network connectivity to our transmitter site. Higher frequency links are available and come with a higher bandwidth, but these are unlicensed and not protected. Theoretically, someone else could interfere with it and knock us off the air

MC: When designing your STL, evaluate your data stream requirements and financially weigh the costs associated with the available types. An example would be to compare a point-to-point T1, capable of 1.5 Mbs., with a microwave system. Keep in mind that it is possible for one microwave path to deliver the same band width capacity as 29 T1 connections.

CK: Until recently, wireless links were limited to operate on the 950 MHz band only and were one-directional. This worked well for a long time. But as the 950 MHz band has become more and more crowded, it is harder to get one of those frequencies. The new links are bidirectional and operate between the 5.8 GHz 23GHz band, and are unlicensed so there are no regulatory issues, and the bandwidth is 100mb or better. If you can convert your audio source to IP, than these links will work.

MC: Simple audio feeds that utilize smaller bandwidths are being replaced with microwave systems capable of large bandwidths to accommodate HD1 and 2 for both audio and data links. Adding an HD2 signal to an existing HD is significantly easier if a larger bandwidth link is available.

Geography and Redundancy:

MC: The line-of-sight is also crucial and for microwave links this will dictate where dishes can be located. For C-Band or KU-Band down links, an unobstructed line-of-sight to the southern horizon is necessary.

ES: For our STL's, we look for high geography and shooting over bodies of water. We prefer paths that are less than 10 miles.

MC: *Because redundancy is also a consideration, it is best to have two discrete systems.* One approach is utilizing the microwave as the primary, and T1 as a back up. In my experience, the microwave link will be much more reliable than the phone line. Another cost-effective backup alternative for your STL is to consider utilizing an ISDN line which may be dependant available in your market.

ES: For a secondary or tertiary path, we will use a T1 line or an ISDN line in an emergency.

Back Up Generator
CBS Radio
Baltimore

What are the Top Priorities for the Technical Operations Center?

General:

ES: *Put the money into the infrastructure.* It's what you are going to be living with for the next 10 or 15 years, and it needs to be bullet-proof. We try to put the money into items that are not easily replaceable and need to be the most reliable. We like to see the TOC centrally located to the studios and big enough to handle the requirements of the current installation and future growth.

MC: It is a common misunderstanding to assume that as technology advances equipment is becoming smaller, more efficient, and that less rack space will be required. On the contrary, because of HD2, more equipment rack space is required. Additional floor space for future equipment should be included in the planning and design of a TOC.

ES: It used to be with your typical AM/FM radio station that you only had to worry about two signals. This has grown to five or six signals and you now have to consider the analog, HD, HD2, streaming, and in some cases HD3 chains. All of these services require digital storage for programming sources, carrier generation for HD channels and streaming services. The way we like to approach it is: *Do not build a TOC for the way you operate today.* The TOC will most likely grow half as much, and in some cases they will be twice your current needs. Where possible, we go with taller racks to cut down on the number and overall footprint of the TOC. We place equipment that we do not have to touch at the top—like STL transmitters or LAN links. You can grow vertically or horizontally.

MC: A complete equipment rack layout is a crucial tool when designing a TOC. You should allow additional floor space for expansion.

ES: The TOC should have its own cooling system independent from the facility and have a redundant system to work as a backup when the primary fails. The equipment just cannot be without cooling.

CK: Recently, the HVAC requirements for the TOC have gone up. This is not because equipment produces more heat but because there is just more equipment in the TOC and less in the studios. This is primarily due to the recent conversion to router-based systems.

ES: Security is a factor for the TOC and access must be limited. Card key access on a monitored system works the best. In addition, the TOC is becoming the facilities computer server room and there are strict guidelines (SarbOx; July 30, 2002) that we have to abide by. This has caused us to reconsider how the TOC and equipment racks are secured.

Grounding:

CK: Grounding in general is a critical issue. *The transmission equipment and equipment racks should be bonded to each other and out to the tower.* The last thing you want is one piece of equipment at one ground potential and another piece of equipment at a different ground potential.

MC: Equipment grounding is crucial and should be carefully designed, detailed, executed, and tested. A star ground system that keeps your tower, electrical service, generator, and electronics at the same ground potential is vital. If this is not the case, you will be susceptible to lightning

ES: Grounding considerations for radio stations, specifically the studios has changed. Grounding used to be provided to ensure the quietest analog signal… no hum, no buzz, or ground loops. Grounding is now provided to prevent accidental static discharges to the equipment. Everything is computer-based; you just can't risk a static discharge wiping out file or a server. I like to see a static dissipative tile with a copper strap back to the main station ground.

Uninterrupted Power Source (UPS):

MC: The financial benefit and applicability of a large central UPS vs. an individual rack-based UPS system is usually determined by the facility size. Small compact UPS systems tend to be less reliable, so the quality and condition of power should be carefully considered. The added benefit of a large central UPS is that power is conditioned. With a bypass switch you can quickly convert between public utility services and the UPS power source. In addition, this system can isolate the station's electronics from lightning.

CK: One of the most important things to consider when designing a TOC is to have the right central UPS. The discrete rack mounted units will eventually fail when you need them. With the right central UPS, batteries can swapped and maintenance performed without any interruptions, so this is a key decision for management to make. Keep in mind that the UPS eliminates reboot time for computers. Potential damage to files that could cause the signal to go off the air is eliminated.

ES: The UPS eliminates reboot time for computers, damaging files, and the signal to go off the air. The UPS only needs to be big enough to operate the equipment until the back-up generator is brought on line. There are systems that are scalable so the UPS can grow as your needs grow in both power capacity and run time. These systems are also hot swappable. If there is a partial failure in the UPS you don't lose everything and batteries can be replaced on the fly. We usually have a UPS in the TOC with discrete ones in the studios. They are all tied together on our computer network and monitored on a regular basis.

What Are Your Primary Considerations for Integration?

General Integration:

CK: *You have to integrate IP and Engineering. They can't be separate because it all goes hand-in-hand.*
The use of an integrator depends first on cost and second on finding someone you are comfortable with. The problem with using an integrator as opposed to doing it in-house is that once the integrator is done, they're gone. Even though every good professional integrator will provide documentation, the local engineer does not always know why things were run in a certain way, and this can lead to problems down the road.

MC: Good integrators are becoming very, very difficult to find. There is not enough consistent work to keep them in business. There may be significant cost benefits to utilizing a local integrator, but finding one with the right qualifications is rare. Most out-of-town firms do not like to be on location for more than two weeks at a time, and this is difficult to schedule as a part of a large project.

ES: The days of self-integrating are all but gone for a couple of reasons. There is no learning-curve time; most young engineers getting into radio now have never integrated an analog or digital facility. The thing about self-integrating is that it is great if you have the time and the skilled labor to do it. What we are finding out is that where we have the skilled labor we don't have the time; or where we have the time, we don't have the skilled labor. Where we have both, we end up killing the engineering staff.

MC: When using an integrator, the most important thing to have is a detailed scope of work that is clearly defined. There is a significant advantage to initially bidding the integration package. The decision to go with a fixed fee or negotiating a time-and-materials basis is project-specific. I don't think there is a right or wrong answer.

ES: Look for an integrator experienced with the infrastructure you will be installing and a proven track record. They will pick up things that the local engineer will forget and they stay focused on the details. You want to make sure they handle everything; we look for a turnkey installation. You can craft an RFP and the RFQ to any scope that you want. The most basic need is to fit out the TOC and tie-lines to the studios, and have the infrastructure up and running and ready to accept audio. The other extreme is a turnkey that includes everything from the STL transmitter to setting mike booms. We have done it both ways.

MC: Some radio groups bring in engineering staff from other markets, but a large build-out can cause hardships at the stations they leave. Other facilities make their engineering staff build out the studios in their spare time.

CK: For integration, everything is going to AES (Audio Engineering Society) and EBU (European Broadcasting Union) digital audio standards. Category 5 cabling is within the impedance standard and is cheap. A few manufacturers are now producing a twisted single pair cable that meets Category 5 standards and 100 ohm impedance, making it possible to run AES audio with the cable. This cable is incredibly cheap to purchase and easy to work with.

MC: Years ago you picked out your studio furniture and someone came in, crawled under it and wired it. Today integrators and broadcast equipment manufacturers are producing more turnkey systems and the industry is heading towards more plug-and-play systems.

CK: From a wiring standpoint, anticipate the future, When considering equipment, and where applicable, the less moving parts the better.

MC: If time is important or you are short of staff, I highly recommend the purchasing of the pre-wire harnesses for all your consoles and routers. These are custom to length, labeled, documented, and fully tested.

Studio Integration:

MC: Studio computers tend to have a shorter life expectancy in the hot and dusty space under studio furniture. One option to address this problem is to locate studio computers in the clean cool TOC environment. This reduces noise and heat load on the studio, extends CPU life expectancy, and both the TOC equipment and Studio CPU'S are on the same UPS system. A keyboard, mouse, and monitor extender system can also allow remote access to all CPU's on the system. When a jock is having computer problems during a show, the fix is remote and the broadcast isn't interrupted. All of the software upgrades are done behind the scenes and really help out with trouble-shooting to have the ability to do it remotely.

ES: I have seen computers centrally consolidated in the TOC, and at other facilities they are dispersed in the studios. This is an engineer's cultural preference. Some believe that with the computers all in one room they are easily maintained, and noise is removed from the studio. *If you design the studio furniture correctly with computers in mind, there is no wrong way to go.* Either technique has its advantages and disadvantages. I personally prefer the computers in the studio. Everything is self-contained. Keep in mind that KVM cabling represents another point of failure and an additional expense.

CK: For studio computers, we have moved away from remote keyboard, mouse, and video links back to the TOC. Initially, these computers were loud and you could not have them in a studio with an open mike. Some of the newer computers have larger volume fans at a lower RPM and are much quieter. There is no longer a sound issue that necessitates the 3 A.M. phone call with a locked up automation system. It is easier to tell them to look to their left and hit the reset button rather then guiding them through the TOC to reset the computer and than run back to the studio to make sure it is rebooting.

CK: Provide for enough data drops into the air studio in particular, or a production studio. These work areas will contain automation computers, a computer for the phone, a computer for remote control, another for the Internet, and a computer for log notes and text.

MC: The changes in technology are allowing for smaller and fewer conduits. However, I would suggest you keep the future in mind and realize *it is very difficult to pull additional cable through a conduit that already has cable installed.*

CK: It is also very important to have microphone and microphone processor consistency throughout the facility. This helps with voice tracking and coordinates the work done in the air and production studios. There should also be a difference between studio microphones used for voiced tracking and live production versus microphones used in a creative studio by production staff who know how to use a condenser type microphone to create a higher quality product.

MC: *Wherever possible, the studios should have the same equipment and electronic set-up.* When the equipment is identical, a jock can switch studios without a learning curve. When there is a failure in a studio, they can walk over to the next studio and pick up where they left off. With current software, user settings can be saved as profiles that can be pulled up in any studio. Before every studio had a different set up, and from a support standpoint, it was difficult to resolve problems and make transitions. Having identical studios also helps limit the complaints from jocks regarding what equipment the other studios have.

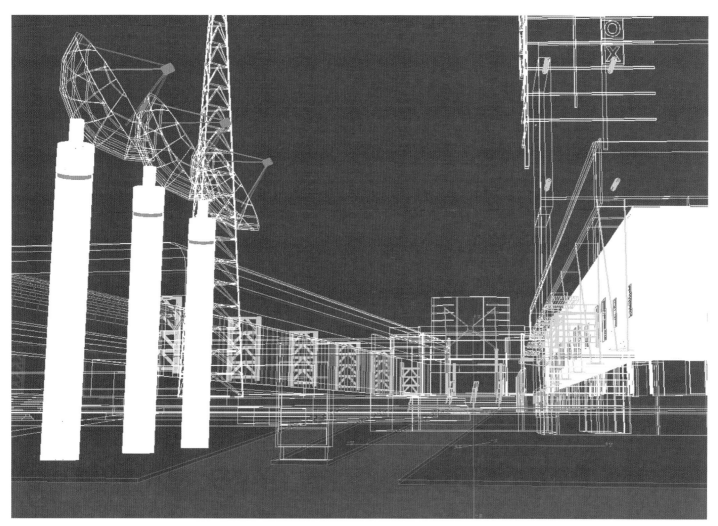

3D Rendering
Cox Radio
Orlando

What are your Design Criteria for On Air and Production Studios?

ES: *Simplicity, uniformity, and versatility are our design goals for studios today. The cleaner and more versatile the studio the better.* With the new digital platforms, any studio can perform any function at any time.

MC: The design and layout of studios is based upon the market and your situation. If you have a strong talent, their needs will have to be considered. I recommend involving your air personalities in the design of their studios. This avoids many problems after you move them in and they feel like they had input.

CK: For studio furniture and equipment, we work towards a clean look. *Reduce the amount of visible equipment by getting it under the counter or behind the host.* And most importantly, improve the site lines between the host and guest.

ES: When we design studios now, we don't design them for a particular purpose. They're all the same and they will handle any steady broadcast scenario–music, multi-talent morning show, or syndicated. With digital systems, you can access any piece of equipment in the facility and pull it up in any studio. From a maintenance standpoint, we can put any studio on the air. This gives us tremendous flexibility in doing primary maintenance.

MC: Here in Kansas City, production studios are right next to the station's air studio with a window between. Initially this was just a small room used for call screening and producing. This has become a dual-purpose studio and allows the production of a show in the morning with a face-to-face line-of-sight with the jock. In the afternoon, it is used as a production studio or for voice tracking.

CK: Production studios in larger markets are getting smaller in size. Usually one production studio is sized and equipped to function as a temporary air studio. Certainly, router and computer automation technologies have allowed this to happen.

MC: The layout and routing of conduit for pulling cabling and access to cable trays for upgrades and maintenance are a priority. *If renovating an existing facility, verify that the existing structures will accommodate sound isolating and other broadcast-related assemblies.*

What Do You Take Into Consideration When Deciding to Reuse Existing Broadcast Equipment, and What Are Your Recycling Options?

ES: When considering reusing equipment, you have to consider useful life and support. We are pretty good at running out equipment assets. By the time we renovate a facility, most equipment is at or beyond life expectancies and has no book value. To remove and reinstall an analog console today is ludicrous. If you have to reuse legacy equipment to meet a budget, it should be the peripheral stuff that is easily replaceable, and put the money into the infrastructure.

CK: *Some of the consoles can be reused at the transmitter site as a temporary studio for disaster recovery.* Microphones and microphone processors are a good candidate for reusing. Reel-to-reel machines and cart machines are dead technologies and there is no reuse.

ES: We are taking disaster recovery plans very seriously. To provide these services, we will re-purpose the equipment and relocate it at the transmitter site, and establish a temporary emergency studio. This equipment will also be distributed throughout the company for this purpose. Because we are located in a multi-tenant building, we are vulnerable and emergencies happen. We work very hard to have back-up servers and studios in case of an emergency.

MC: Almost every facility that has gone through a build-out has had used equipment that had value when it was decommissioned. But after it sits around for a year or so it is useless. I get a lot of offers to take the old equipment; the problem is that no one wants to pay for it. Occasionally, an integrator will buy the old equipment or trade it for services. More often than not, other corporate facilities will request the old equipment and it will be sent to their facility. E-Bay is another option, but the problem with that are the manpower requirements to crate and ship the equipment.

CK: Studio equipment has a life expectancy. If there are several years left, it should be reused and, we try to see if other markets need the equipment. And if that doesn't work out, we have put equipment up on E-Bay.

ES: We have also traded equipment for services. Recently, we had to exit one of our old facilities quickly. For the trouble and cost of removing the equipment we donated it to a smaller market station. They came in and removed the equipment and loved getting it. That makes everybody happy. Occasionally we donate the equipment. This is a good will gesture to broadcasting schools and colleges.

What Do You Look for During Construction and What is the Best Way to Avoid Oversights?

MC: 1. Hire a competent design team who has experience and knows what they are doing.
2. If possible, it helps to hire a contractor who has experience building broadcast facilities.
3. Walk the site daily, take photographs and discuss discrepancies. If you don't understand what is going on, *ask*, because the next day it may be covered up.
4. If your contractor has not installed a studio door and the budget allows, have the door manufacturer come on site and train the general contractor. Once the door is installed, you have to live with it. You have one shot to get it right, and going back to fix the problem is almost impossible.

CK: 1. *Read the plans! Read the plans! Read the plans!*
2. You want an architect at the very least with experience building soundproof rooms and better yet, an architect with experience building a broadcast facility.
3. Have a qualified contractor with similar experience.
4. During construction, walk through the site regularly. If you are not sure about something, ASK!

ES: 1. Make sure that long lead items are identified and ordered as early as possible.
2. The greatest help is an experienced architect familiar with radio station facilities, knows how they operate, and understands the follow-up. Even with all of my experience in the radio broadcast industry, there are things the architect will pick up, and brings lessons learned from other projects to apply them to your project. This makes the job go a whole lot smoother.
3. Make sure the contractor has experience building broadcast studios and that they understand what is required and understand the importance of following the drawings.
4. *Visit the job site as much as possible.* Take photographs as it's being built. Appearing on the job site daily as it is being constructed is priceless.

What are a few ideas that would reduce equipment and facility maintenance?

MC: 1. Reduce the number and individual types of light bulbs. Use readily available standard light bulbs. Some bulbs can be very expensive and difficult to find.
 2. Install corner guards at major corridors.
 3. Occupancy lighting controls are a big plus. They cut down on energy use, and simplify end-of-the-day shut down.
 4. Any effort that would simplify or reduce regular maintenance of mechanical systems would be appreciated.

CK: 1. Build to expand. You should try to build for 15 years down the road, as this is the typical life of the facility The problem is that technology is changing so fast that it is hard to envision changes more than five years out.
 2. Make sure that all cabling is labeled and documented.
 3. IP is where everything is going. *The fewer moving parts the better.*

ES: 1. Use hard surface floors where ever possible.
 2. Install floor drains in bathrooms.
 3. Simplify changing HVAC filters and getting better access to them. I like preventative maintenance items.
 4. Use more efficient light fixtures and controls to reduce operating cost.
 5. For generator maintenance, we mandate that the generator be regularly inspected and tested. When we need these systems, they had better work and run for the required period of time.

Design and Photo Credits

p 103   Entrance Stair
             Entercom Communications
             Kansas City, Kansas
             Source: Bloomfield & Associates, Architects
             Photographer: © Stephen Swalwell

p 105   Back-Up Generator
             CBS Radio
             Baltimore, Maryland
             Source: Bloomfield & Associates, Architects

p 111   3D Rendering
             Cox Radio
             Orlando, Florida
             Source: Bloomfield & Associates, Architects

Meeting Room

Entercom Communications
Kansas City, Kansas
Bloomfield & Associates, *Architects*
Photographer: © Stephen Swalwell

Air Studio Lighting

Entercom Communications
Kansas City

chapter seven

materials and illumination: the theater of radio

Perhaps the most compelling aspect of radio its ability to captivate the senses. Magically through sound the shadows of taste, touch, smell, and sight are questioned and brought to the fore. The selection and design of materials and lighting for your facility should capture this magic --- the theater of radio.

The selection of materials and lighting is also the physical manifestation of the station's vision. How your facility is perceived by clients, guests, and staff (whether a brief first impression or a daily encounter) should be a memorable, positive and lasting experience.

This section will present material and lighting considerations that are specific to broadcast facilities. Whether a new station from the ground up or extensive renovation, they typically are made from similar lighting and material palates. It is the manner by which they are assembled and deployed throughout the facility, in a budget conscious way, that can form a unique and supportive work place.

Material Selection

Material selection falls into two categories:

- Products that are specifically needed to support their particular function
- Products that contribute to establishing the station's public image and are integrated into the performance of the overall effort

The chasm between them is not wide. But budgetary Considerations will, of course, come into play. An important issue to consider is long-term cost vs. short-term expense. Your architect and mechanical engineer will advise you on such aspects as the rate-of-return values, life expectancy, and maintenance considerations for a variety of systems and materials. They will find solutions best suited to meet your station's needs.

Similarly, there are finish materials that cost more initially but have longer wear value. Flooring materials offer a good example of choice options. Stone, rubber, ceramic tile, hardwood, or other hard flooring types will often cost two to three times as much as a good carpet but may last three to four times as long. (*A note of caution*: when selecting flooring, be aware of slick surfaces where employees or visitors may slip and fall.)

Even if the station could afford high-end materials throughout the facility, the issues of maintenance, noise, and comfort dictate the use of more expensive materials in areas that receive high traffic or wear. These include major public spaces: halls, lobbies, kitchens, and printing and mail centers.

Elevator Lobby Floor
Entercom Communications
New Orleans

Local Materials

Consider for use the locally produced products-either manufactured or raw materials-true to the region in which the station is based. Depending on the station's overall image, these materials must also be appropriate to the design concept. When they can be incorporated into the design program, their selection will be regarded as supportive of local industry. Their use can encourage the radio station's status as an integral part of the community it serves.

Time was that local materials had an impact on the design of facilities. Pride of place had something to do with it as did the skills and talents of local trades persons. This is less the case today. The considerate planner will take local materials into account as part of the building program.

As an added benefit, using local materials may also allow for some savings in the cost of materials and shipping.

Wall Panel Detail
Entercom Communications
Denver

Small Conference Area
Entercom Communications
Denver

Sustainability

A few simple efforts in the area of energy conservation are usually the cheapest and quickest way to reduce operation costs in a broadcast facility. It is also the cleanest way to decrease the already overburdened electrical grid. In this way, both the corporate bottom line and concerns for the planet are served.

The ability to operate the facility in a manner that is cost-efficient from an energy consumption standpoint should be integral to the entire process. Start with the selection of a team of professionals who are experienced and sensitive to this issue and continue through site selection and building systems design. If the goal is to stay in place and upgrade, often a few simple improvements or changes can significantly reduce operating costs.

"The building sector has a tremendous impact on the environment. In 2002 there were... nearly five million commercial buildings in the United States. According to the U.S. Department of Energy (DOE), buildings in the United States consume more than 37% of our total energy and 68% of our electricity annually. Five billion gallons of potable water are used to flush toilets daily. A typical North American commercial construction project generates up to 2.5 pounds of solid waste per square foot of floor space."

The U.S. Green Building Council

Do not hesitate to investigate local, regional, and even national incentives for building with a concern for energy consumption. Often these are simple items that can be included in the design and construction of the new facility and have a relatively small impact on the cost of the project. Typically these efforts have a very fast investment return rate.

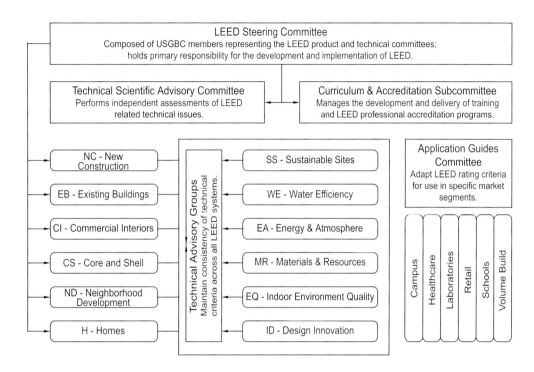

LEED Steering Committee
Composed of USGBC members representing the LEED product and technical committees; holds primary responsibility for the development and implementation of LEED.

Technical Scientific Advisory Committee
Performs independent assessments of LEED related technical issues.

Curriculum & Accreditation Subcommittee
Manages the development and delivery of training and LEED professional accreditation programs.

NC - New Construction

EB - Existing Buildings

CI - Commercial Interiors

CS - Core and Shell

ND - Neighborhood Development

H - Homes

Technical Advisory Groups
Maintain consistency of technical criteria across all LEED systems.

SS - Sustainable Sites

WE - Water Efficiency

EA - Energy & Atmosphere

MR - Materials & Resources

EQ - Indoor Environment Quality

ID - Design Innovation

Application Guides Committee
Adapt LEED rating criteria for use in specific market segments.

Campus
Healthcare
Laboratories
Retail
Schools
Volume Build

LEED Structural Organization Chart (Leadership in Energy and Environmental Design)
Rexel Electrical & Datacom Products

Selecting a "Sustainable Site"

Whether looking to build new or lease and renovate to suit, the issues associated with sustainable design go well beyond simply increasing insulation and using energy efficient equipment. The subject is very complex and includes a broad spectrum of issues that start with how and where the new facility will sit and whether staff can access the site by using "alternative transportation" such as public transit. In the realm of new construction, the site can have a significant impact on initial costs and just how "green" your building and site development can be. *Even in projects that involve renovation, site selection will have an impact on both cost and your ability to satisfy an agenda that is at least partially based on a concern for the environment.*

When building new or reconfiguring a site, don't forget about issues such as ground coverage and water-efficient landscaping. Often local codes will determine some of this but, typically, they do not go very far on issues of sustainability.

If you are reworking your existing facility or just concerned with your energy consumption in general, start with an "energy audit." Ask the design professionals to visit the site and review existing conditions.

This survey should address a wide variety of issues that can range from highly tangible items such us local utility cost structures to an analysis of these costs and the efficiency of existing heating and cooling systems. On a less tangible basis, the survey can look at day cycles and associated space use, examine existing equipment such as lighting fixtures from both an efficiency standpoint as well as the quality of light provided. The condition of exterior walls and windows can be evaluated as part of the survey findings.

Simple interventions on the facade have reduced both heat gain and sun glare in the studios. This was achieved while also providing a new and appropriate image for this six station cluster in Greenville.

Building Facade
before (above)
after (below)
Entercom Communications
Greenville

Designing In and Out of the Box
Designing a building shell with a concern for environmental issues typically is a regionalized activity. By and large, energy saving criteria that work well on a north-facing site in Minnesota will not hold true for the west façade of a building in Orlando. While most Americans are acquainted with the value of insulation and storm windows, this effort is just a beginning in the process.

Typically, most studio and office environments require some internal cooling on even the coldest of days. The trick is to reduce those needs to as low a level as possible and still maintain an appropriate comfort factor for staff.

Accordingly, the first line of defense is to keep temperature extremes outside the shell of the building. Sizing windows and appropriate shading devices is a start. The simple act of designing an "air lock" at the entry(s) will not only reduce the loss of tempered air but increase the comfort factor of the receptionist.

There are many other areas that contribute to the making of "sustainable space." For example, design-whether new or renovation-that allows for daylighting and views for as many employees as possible can decrease the need for artificial lighting and increase the comfort factor.

Simple items such as low-volume water fixtures can save a great deal over time. In some communities, on site showers have been found to effectively encourage staff to ride bicycles to work this not only saves on fossil fuels but presumable makes for a healthier employee! Encourage your architect to give this area priority.

Material Selection and the Construction Process
The value of reusing and reworking certain parts of a building is often unclear until the project is well underway. Often large contractors prefer and find it cost-effective to remove everything and start over. But as dumping fees and labor costs continue to rise, this is becoming less common.

What is clear is that reusing as much as possible decreases the burden on our already bursting landfills. In addition, there are more and more materials readily available that have a recycled content in excess of fifty percent. Using these materials need not increase costs significantly. Drywall is a good start as are carpet, floor tile, and ceramic tile.

When selecting materials, your design professionals should be able to recommend a wide variety of materials that satisfy the demands of using recycled products. They should also take into account what is involved with producing the material and getting it to the site.

Specifying wood species that are rapidly renewable is another way. Select, if possible, materials that are produced within a tight radius of the site–say two hundred miles–which saves on delivery costs. Use fewer fossil fuels and disperse less of their associated pollutants.

Let the decision to build or renovate in a manner that is energy-efficient be part of the station branding. It may help attract both listeners as well as advertisers. A well-designed work environment is also a terrific way to attract staff.

Illuminating the Broadcast Facility

William M. Kader, IESNA
Grenald Waldron Associates
Narberth, Pennsylvania

Lighting helps accentuate form, identify structures, and define hierarchy. It creates mood and allows people to carry out the tasks required for their role within the facility.

Broadcast facilities are comprised of spaces and working environments that are both typical to most organizations and distinctive to the broadcasting industry. Storage areas, administrative spaces, private offices, conference rooms, production studios, editing suites, and green rooms are all incorporated in the modern broadcast facility. Each of these spaces requires a unique lighting approach to make it functional as well as distinctive.

Many factors enter into the decisions determining proper illumination levels for broadcast facilities.

- the type of work being performed
- hours of operation
- occupant preferences
- the average age of the employees

A professional lighting designer with experience in the design of the varied elements that make up a modern broadcast facility is a valuable member of the design team. Lighting designers mix art and science to produce a creative look by understanding the properties of light and knowing how and where to apply them. The lighting designer's program includes an understanding of the design team's objectives, the physical nature of the building, and the needs of the owner.

Conference Room/Open Office
Ferry Building
San Francisco

Work Area Lighting
Entercom Communications
Kansas City

Balancing Needs and Wants

The lighting designer must create an exceptionally illuminated environment that fulfills the architectural requirements, is maintenance-friendly, and above all, meets the budget.

The differences between the owner's ideas and the requirements of the facility often include budgetary vs. programmatic divergences. For example, the owner may want all lamps specified in the fixtures to be compact fluorescent or metal halide to help reduce maintenance and operation costs. However, the facility may require incandescent or halogen sources to best meet the unique functions of the space and accommodate the tasks to be performed.

Conversely, the owner may insist on theatrical or intelligent lighting fixtures because of the perceived importance of space. These may require unique control systems and typically cost more than conventional fixtures. If the overall construction budgets cannot afford such amenities, it's up to the lighting designer to generate options that balance these needs and wants.

In addition to maintaining a close rapport with the design team, the lighting designer should arrange to meet with facility staff to gauge their specific lighting needs. Because broadcast facilities are diverse in nature, the lighting designer, in conjunction with the design team, must be open to a variety of solutions for a range of applications. Solutions that work for office staff may not necessarily work for technicians or the on-air talent.

General Lighting and the Work Environment

The recommended illuminance levels for offices range from 30 to 60 foot-candles. This figure is subject to individual evaluation, as the quality of the visual environment has a substantial impact on the "appropriate" amount of illumination. In well-designed office spaces, with light-colored surfaces, appropriate task lighting, and careful placement of lights and furniture to avoid glare and shadows, much lower illuminance levels are acceptable, and may even be preferred by the occupants.

Open Office Lighting

Lighting for open offices should be designed to provide visibility for typical paper-based and electronic tasks while enhancing the environment's sense of light and space. These areas, typically. consist of low-height partition walls that create cubicles and individual work stations with computer terminals. A well-designed office space involves the careful placement of lights and furniture to avoid glare and shadows, using color-correlated surfaces and lamps.

Open Office
The Finish Line
Indianapolis

Work Environment
Peerless Lighting
San Francisco

The most appropriate and comfortable method for illuminating these areas is through the use of indirect fluorescent fixtures suspended from the ceiling. Indirect lighting provides a soft, even distribution of light by using the ceiling to reflect light. This method reduces glare on computer monitors and provides the best visual comfort for tasks associated with these environments.

Critical to any indirect lighting design is the finish of the surfaces from which the light will be reflected. Ceilings and walls should be white or finished in reflective tones that help distribute the lighting evenly throughout the space.

Indirect lighting, however, does require sufficient ceiling height to accommodate the pendant-hung fixtures and allow even distribution of the light. In areas with lower ceilings, there are specialty fixtures that provide indirect lighting. These fixtures should be carefully laid out and provide adequate coverage and distribution of light.

Where the ceiling height does not allow for suspended indirect lighting, recessed fluorescent troffers or indirect "basket" type fixtures will typically be specified. These provide a similar lighting appearance as indirect pendants but with slightly less glare control. They are convenient because they can be integrated into less expensive acoustic ceiling tile systems, and cost effective because they can be used throughout the space.

In all open office areas, task lighting should be used to light the work surfaces. Adding visual interest, such as halogen or metal halide accent lights on architectural features, helps break up the flat and sometimes unexciting lighting that is typical with fluorescent sources. They can also be used to identify corridors or entrances.

Indirect Fixture   *Troffer Fixture*   *Task Lighting*

Private Offices

Enclosed or private offices can again be illuminated using indirect or "basket" type fluorescent luminaires. In addition, lighting walls separately will create visual interest through the use of compact fluorescent wallwash, or if appropriate, halogen wallwash luminaires.

Dimming adds an extra layer of lighting dimension to offices and gives the occupants an opportunity to vary the levels of lighting in the room depending on the task.

Push-button wall switches with preset lighting "scenes" are the easiest way for occupants to go to a dim level when needed but still be able to restore to previously desired higher levels of light. These controls can also include sound and motion occupancy sensors that will turn the lights off after a programmed length of time for energy efficiency.

Conference Rooms

The lighting systems for conference/meeting areas should accommodate the needs of guest speakers as well as general staff. Today's presentation technology often includes digital and video formats.

The ambient lighting of the conference room should be dimmable. Indirect or louvered fluorescent fixtures will minimize glare and provide a range of lighting levels suitable for note-taking during slide presentations and reading paper copy during presentations.

Separately controlled fluorescent lighting at the perimeter of the room will define the edges of the space and provide highlighting for marker board or pin-up presentations. In spaces with video conference requirements, supplemental lighting will enhance vertical light levels to optimize the quality of the transmitted images.

Preset dimming controls can be provided to vary the lighting levels for the various A/V requirements and functions of these rooms.

Conference Room
CBS Radio
Baltimore

Lobbies and Common Areas

On any given day, broadcast facilities play host to a wide variety of guests, ranging from important celebrities, to major advertisers, to students, and general audience members. The station will be visited for interviews, signings, and tours.

Lobbies, reception areas, cafeterias, and green rooms play an important role in helping to market the organization by creating a lasting first impression on visitors. More often, the finishes and materials used in the construction of the walls, floors, and ceilings of these spaces are a finer quality than those in the rest of the building. Lighting plays a crucial role in emphasizing these architectural distinctions, and in creating a warm and welcoming environment. The decorative and functional lighting fixtures should be architecturally integral to the space.

Lobby
ACE Limited
Hamilton, Bermuda

For lobbies and reception areas, feature walls may be the background for station logos, awards, and memorabilia. If the layout of these walls is not permanent and is expected to change through the life of the facility, adjustable track lighting may be a flexible solution. Accent lighting should draw guests to the displays that are important.

Accent lighting on walls, doorways, seating areas and reception desks together with a lower level of general ambient lighting creates an interesting space. Often, these rooms are used for gatherings and events, so multiple zone dimming systems are preferred to set appropriate mood. These dimmable circuits can help to reduce daytime energy loads when linked to a building management system.

Green rooms often reflect a more playful feel. Colorful pendants, ultra-modern track lighting or backlit ceiling or wall panels might be used here. The use of dimmable circuits might be implemented here to help establish varying moods for the room and the guests.

Studio and Production Space Lighting

Lobby Atrium
The International House
Philadelphia

Lobby
CPM Media
San Francisco

The nature of studio and production spaces varies greatly between broadcast facilities Depending on how the space is programmed and if there will be live telecasts, web casts, or live radiocasts, the lighting design fulfills specific users needs.

In large production studios where events are aired live or taped for televised broadcast, a flexible lighting grid should be included. The system should allow for fixtures to be secured in any position for lighting sets and to provide key, back, fill, and cyc lighting.

Dimmed circuits distributed conveniently throughout the grid allow for the location of lighting equipment controlled by a master console or handheld devices.

The quantity of dimmed circuits is based on the size of the room and the production needs of the facility. Dimmers should be remotely located outside of the production spaces to eliminate

dimmer noise, and hum and be closely coordinated to avoid interference with the audio system.

Studio lighting equipment is rarely static, and the positions of the lighting fixtures can change regularly. Fixtures are taken down and put up, focused and refocused, raised and lowered based on the needs of the set or the shoot.

Lamps used in these fixtures range from tungsten/halogen to fluorescent to HID and HMI sources. Each of these light sources provides a unique correlated color temperature of light ranging from 2800°K to 8000°K.

Although the director of photography typically has the final say in the lighting decisions, most studios use 3000-3500°K lamps for interior spaces and cooler ranges for exterior spots.

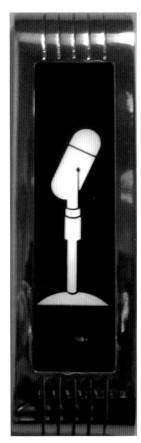

On-Air Fixture

Light Sources and Technical Considerations

Unique lighting needs apply to radio studios which do not involve video taping and they require less lighting equipment but still have unique lighting requisites.

Within the on-air studios, the talent is typically situated at a console with microphones and video monitors. The illumination here uses dimmable and adjustable lighting fixtures with good glare control. Track lighting with barn doors or snoots over the console with supplemental recessed down lighting throughout the room is a popular solution.

Pod casts or web casts emanating from these Air Studios need different lighting to fulfill these needs. Each talent position should be lit separately. Key lighting, back-lighting, and background fill will create dimension within the frames of the shot.

Call-in radio shows require the air talent to have direct view of the call screeners who are usually in an adjoining room behind a glass window. The position of the light fixtures in these rooms is crucial. The lighting needs to be balanced between the rooms to eliminate glare and contrast so that the on-air talent can see the faces of the call screeners.

All of the lighting within the air studios and the call screeners' rooms should be on dimmed circuits. This approach also applies to news formats that require direct line of sight between air talent and newsroom.

Avoid a "one lamp fits all" approach to broadcast facilities! Possible long-life sources solutions are:

- fluorescent lamps
- HID (high-intensity discharge) lamps
- occupancy sensors
- daylight harvesting devices incorporated with the building management systems.

Fluorescent Lamps

Long-life fluorescent sources operating on high frequency electronic ballasts are excellent for providing ambient lighting in open offices, private offices, and conference rooms. They are relatively inexpensive to replace and have a life expectancy of between 15,000 to 30,000 hours.

Fluorescent lighting systems use less wattage to produce required lighting levels and therefore produce less heat which helps reduce ongoing HVAC costs. When coordinated with the MEP, fluorescent lighting systems can reduce lighting loads by as much as 60 percent, significantly reducing the size and cost of electrical and mechanical equipment.

The typical fluorescent lamp is either T5 or T8 type with a correlated color temperature of 3500°K and a color rendering index of at least 75. Compact fluorescent lamps should have a correlated color temperature of 3500°K to provide a continuity of source color. The final color temperature of the lamps needs to be coordinated with the design team and balanced with other light sources used in the design.

Fluorescent lamps often contain impurities that can affect their operation. To neutralize these impurities, operate the lamps at full intensity for 100 hours (also known as "seasoning" the lamps).

Fluorescent lamps cannot be dimmed without including a dimmable ballast as part of the fixture specification. These add a huge amount of flexibility to the lighting design, but dimmable ballasts are not cheap. Between the cost of the upgraded ballast and the subsequent, control system required, the material cost of the fixtures can sometimes be double to that of a standard fluorescent fixture.

Halogen lamps

Halogen sources give a warmer form of light. With a correlated color temperature of 2700°K, they can provide sparkle and punch where highlighting is needed. Because of higher wattages and heat generally associated with these sources, these lamps should be limited to areas of special interest, such as to highlight artwork and architectural details, or to illuminate conference and green rooms.

Fluorescent Lamp

Halogen Lamp

LED Lamp

Most incandescent and halogen sources are dimmable without the requirement of special equipment and are generally less expensive than fluorescent fixtures. They can be dimmed out-of-the-box with an inexpensive dimmable wall switch or dimming system. Low-voltage halogen fixtures may require a specific low-voltage dimmer and should be verified with the fixture manufacturer.

LED (Light Emitting Diode) Sources
LEDs are at the technological forefront of satisfying the demand for a long-life, low-heat lighting source. Major lighting fixture manufacturers are investing heavily in the research and development of LEDs as a viable light source.

Today, LEDs are used primarily in accent lighting applications such as cove lighting, backlighting, and artwork or graphic lighting. They are also great for direct viewing applications such as pathway marker lights and accent lighting for building exteriors.

With seamless color changing ability and small size, LED fixtures can add an exciting flair to certain applications. One drawback is the cost of LED fixtures and their associated controls and power supplies, which can be quite high relative to conventional fixtures.

Typically, illumination from a LED source is not sufficient to compete with even moderate levels of ambient light, so the designer must be aware of the entire lit environment before LEDs are specified. Often, ambient lighting from LED sources are rendered almost indistinguishable in spaces where fluorescent and HID sources are also present.

Published reports claim that the lamp life of some colors of LED sources can be up to 100,000 hours. Although their application is limited, low energy consumption, long life, and low maintenance may as well be worth the investment. LEDs often pay for themselves in maintenance savings within a few years.

Lighting Controls and Sustainable Design

Lighting Controls

Lighting controls can save energy, save on maintenance cost, and reduce peak demand in offices and other areas of the facility. While saving money, controls also help provide a pleasant atmosphere and allow for a convenient interface with the user. There are several different kinds of controls available. The choice of controls should be based on lighting usage patterns and space use requirements.

Areas with intermittent use are well-suited to occupancy sensors. In large, open office areas with many occupants, scheduled switching or time clocks are often an effective energy-saving strategy. When electricity demand costs are high, advanced lighting controls can be used for demand limiting to reduce lighting loads.

Dimmers

Overall energy consumption of a building can be trimmed by as much as 80 percent with dimmers. They reduce the electrical load directly, and also allow the HVAC system to run more efficiently. Dimming incandescent and halogen lamps on a regular, maintained basis can sometimes increase lamp life by as much as 50 to 75 percent. Dimming fluorescent fixtures, rather than on-and-off switching, extends lamp life by reducing the number of starting surges.

Although not considered necessary in administrative areas such as open and private offices, dimmed lighting fixtures can be quite beneficial. Dimmers permit greater flexibility of the space because the user can vary the light level to better accommodate the tasks being performed.

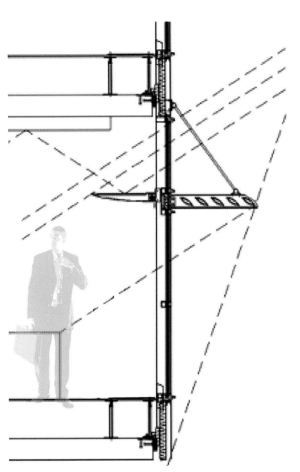

Light Shelf and Sun Shade Detail
Hunter Douglas

Daylighting

In today's energy-conscious environment, the use of daylighting as a functional source of illumination is an important element in newly constructed or totally renovated buildings. A building that is LEED (Leadership in Energy and Environmental Design) certified or identified by the U.S. Green Building Council is fast becoming more desirable to owners. Day-lit offices with properly adjusted daylight sensors with dimming ballasts make sense and certainly save money and energy. However, because of budget constraints or conditions in existing buildings, not all facilities can easily take advantage of natural light.

Light Shelf
Hunter Douglas

Back of House Areas

Lighting for back-of-house areas such as storage, utility and service areas should be designed to support the visual and security requirements of each space. Lensed fluorescent troffers can provide lighting in spaces with finished ceilings. Pendant or chain-hung industrial fluorescent and/or HID (high intensity discharge) systems can be used in areas with exposed structure. Wall-mounted direct/indirect fluorescent lighting can be installed in stairwells.

Low-temperature ballasts and vapor-tight fixtures can be used whenever direct exposure to the elements is unavoidable. Occupancy sensor controls can be incorporated into the lighting for enclosed storage areas. Wall box switches with occupancy sensors are useful as local control in utility and service areas.

Core and service areas such as pantries, copy rooms, and coat areas can be lit inexpensively with recessed fluorescent fixtures, supplemented by under-cabinet task lights where appropriate.

Toilet room lighting can be provided by compact fluorescent down lights, with linear fluorescent wall slots for the vanity and toilet walls.

Training Room
Vangard Campus
Malvern

Maintenance

Facility managers inevitably ask the question whether spot re-lamping or group re-lamping is more appropriate. Group re-lamping, in which a set of lamps is replaced at a scheduled time, rather than spot re-lamping, in which lamps are only replaced when they burn out, is generally the most beneficial approach. For the most part, group re-lamping applies to fluorescent and HID lamps rather than incandescent, which have much shorter lifetimes.

Group re-lamping requires much less labor per lamp than spot re-lamping. A worker might take as long as a half-hour to retrieve and install a single lamp. If all the materials were on hand for a large number of lamps, a worker could move systematically from fixture to fixture and cut the required time to about three minutes per lamp. The process is also less disruptive, as group re-lamping is usually done outside working hours, and it ensures a brighter and more evenly lit work environment.

A popular option for facility managers today is outsourcing the maintenance of the lighting systems to lighting contractors. By helping to reduce scheduling issues, it also reduces the quantity of on-site lamp stocks required.

Conference Room
Endeavor Talent Agency
Beverly Hills

Design and Photo Credits

Additional Resources

– The Green Building Council
http://www.greenbuildingcouncil.com

– Architectural Woodworking Institute
http://www.awinet.org

– The American Institute of Architects
http://www.aia.org

– The Marble Institute of America
http://www.marble-institute.com

– Masonry Institute of America
http://www.masonryinstitute.org

– American Iron and Steel Institute
http://www.steel.org

– Structural Engineering Institute
http://www.seinstitute.org

– The Acoustic Society of America
http://www.acoustics.org

– The Society of Broadcast Engineers
http://www.sbe.org

System Installation
CBS Radio
Baltimore

chapter eight
building systems: what you do not hear

Mechanical, electrical, plumbing, and fire protection systems can absorb up to thirty to forty percent of construction costs on a typical project. It is a common target for cutting costs, even though temperature and humidity comfort may well be the largest complaint from the stuff heard by management. Utility costs can also be a significant component in the operating costs of a facility having a direct impact on the bottom line. *Control these things early so they don't control you later on.*

Unlike much of this book which focuses on the visually accessible and the functional making of space, Chapter 8 is really about what you don't see or hear. More specifically, it focuses on what you do *not* want to see and hear in a well designed broadcast facility. It is also about all the components that ensure comfort for staff and quiet for studios.

The Role of the Mechanical Engineer on the Design Team

Marvin Waxman, PE
Marvin Waxman Consulting Engineers
Philadelphia, Pennsylvania

The briefest answer to the query of "What exactly is the mechanical engineer's responsibility as part of the design team?" is: *"Make the facility work."*

Here's a short list of the scope of the mechanical engineer's responsibilities to the owner, the station manager, the architect, and the users regarding the HVAC (heating, ventilating and air conditioning) system.

- The facility has to be warm enough in the winter and cool enough in the summer to keep the occupants comfortable in their work environment.

- Ducts and air handling equipment must be as seamlessly integrated into the architecture as possible.

- The noise level of the equipment for acoustically sensitive areas of the station must be carefully researched to meet the technical specifications.

- Within the tasks under his direction, the mechanical engineer deals with people, places, and things.

- Establish the load by estimating the heat generated by lights, equipment, and people.

- Estimate the impact of the station's location on the HVAC: upper floor in a high-rise or multi-story building; street level location; or tree–standing building.

- Calculate the interior environment system based on whether the project is new construction or a renovation.

- Make the facility energy-efficient.

- Meet the budget.

Mechanical Construction
Entercom Communications
Greenville

Budget

Early in the design process, the percentage of the overall construction budget that is allocated for the HVAC is established and communicated to the mechanical engineering consultant for system planning. Typically, the range is 30 to 40 percent of the budget. For new construction, the budget is closer to the 40 percent level. For an existing building, where it is possible to use or adapt existing systems, 30 percent can initially be set aside.

In configuring the HVAC budget, the station's decision to occupy space as a tenant in a multi-story building, or to be located in a free-standing structure, is a prime determinant of the system that will meet the broadcaster's performance standards and the capital set-aside.

In any facility where the station is in a multi-use building; the first question is: How much of its HVAC equipment needs can be linked to the structure's existing systems? If it is possible to be tied into the building equipment, how feasible is it to accommodate the station's specific needs?

Unlike many other commercial facilities, most radio stations are 24/7 operations, 365 days a year. Their HVAC equipment is operating continuously. It's an important milestone for station management to compare lower first costs versus long-term savings when making their investment decisions.

Undeniably, more efficient equipment translates into higher first cost. For example, natural gas-powered equipment is cheaper as a base energy source, but the building system to use it would require such items as boilers and flues. Certain chillers for air conditioning use one-half the energy of other brands on the market, but commensurately, their ticket price is higher than the competition's.

Another critical consideration is: What is the station's power failure level? If there is a power outage, how soon does the station need to be back on the air, and what type of back-up equipment will it need to keep it in operation for two hours, four hours, or more? The answers depend on how much is in their financial allocation to give reality to their requirements.

Sometimes, the reality of the budget and what it costs to stay live on the air in the case of an emergency are not the same. *It's up to the mechanical engineer and the other members of the design team to help station management make decisions that balance the monies at their disposal with the station's mission.*

Every radio station embarking on a building project wants the lowest operating cost and the best system that they can buy. Building owners, if not the station, may have a different agenda. For a Philadelphia station, an existing building system was used for office and administrative areas by modifying it to fit the space. Other spaces that were not sound-sensitive but required 24/7 operation were tied into the building system with a station-installed back-up. For studios that were to be operating 24/7 and had special sound criteria, an entire new HVAC system was designed.

Air Studio in Lobby
Entercom Communications
New Orleans

Determining the Load

In any season of the year, the HVAC load in every room is made up of heat-generating lights, office machines such as computers, and the people occupying the space. The more people working in the station, the more ventilation will be required to bring fresh area into the system. This will increase the equipment load.

The first step for the mechanical engineer after establishing the budget is data gathering for every space. Then, a gross dollar number will be calculated to produce a more refined proposal for client review. Information needed from the architect includes space allocations for all of the station's talent, support, and technical personnel, and spaces needed to house all primary and secondary equipment. The architect will also evaluate from interviews with station personnel the level at which critical and non-critical spaces have to be considered for quality of sound transmission and potential growth and expansion.

The lighting designer will submit a preliminary light source and lamp selection schedule for the spaces that comprise the station's various functions, from the lobby to the library.

Based on the projected watts/sq. ft., the estimated lighting load is transmitted to the mechanical engineer. Each studio's schedule is researched, and the ambient and specialty lighting is plotted. Based on these initial plans, the mechanical engineer will develop more refined calculations.

Next, a listing of all the equipment needed to run the station is gathered. From this information, an estimate of the overall mechanical load is developed. A preliminary equipment selection is prepared for primary and back-up systems.

If occupied spaces are to be placed on the perimeter of the building, such as studios or lobbies, the engineer will have to take into consideration the amount of heat that is being generated from the exterior environment. This factor is figured into calculations for the load estimate.

AHU	AREA	Lighting Load	Equipment Load	People Number	People Load (type)	Calculated Cooling Load (Tons)	Ft^2	Air Flow (CFM)	CFM/ft^2
1	Lower Level & Maz	400,000 BTU	100,000 BTU	750	Dining	128.0	11315.0	38284.0	3.38
2	Upper Office	2.0 W/ft^2	0.5 W/ft^2	101	Office	29.7	10364.0	11252.0	1.09
3	STUDIO	2.0 W/ft^2	32250 W	71	Office	34.5	3574.0	14000.0	3.92
4	Upper Level	1.4 W/ft^2	42100 BTU	59	Dining	19.4	5584.0	7642.0	1.37
6	KITCHEN	2.0 W/ft^2	143000 BTU	15	Walking	18.1	2900.0	8316.0	2.87
7	Lower Office	2.0 W/ft^2	0.5 W/ft^2	25	Office	7.2	3796.0	2800.0	0.74
8	OFFICE	2.0 W/ft^2	0.5 W/ft^2	13	Office	3.9	2015.0	1530.0	0.76
TOTAL						241			

STUDIO EQUIPMENT

Air Studio	3 KVA
Master Control	8 KVA
Performance Studio	5 KVA
Performance Control	8 KVA
News Studio	2 KVA
News Control	5 KVA
World Café Control	5 KVA
CD Library and Storage	2 KVA
Engineering Shop	2 KVA
Edit Rooms	3 KVA
Total	43 KVA
Heating Load	32250 W

LOWER LEVEL EQUIPMENT

Amplifier Equipment	60,000 BTU
Lighting Dimmer	40,000 BTU
Total	100,000 BTU

LOWER LEVEL LIGHTING

Above Audience	192,000 BTU
Above Stage	128,000 BTU
on Stage	80,000 BTU
Total	400,000 BTU

KITCHEN EQUIPMENT LOAD

Item	Gas Load (BTU)	HVAC Load (BTU)
48" Char-Broiler	120,000	13,200
Range with Oven	680,000	54,400
Fryer	360,000	7,200
Skillet	144,000	14,400
Steamer	380,000	15,200
Electric Equipment	384,719	38,472
Total	2,068,719	142,872

EQUIPMENT LOAD

Item	Gas Load (BTU)	HVAC Load (BTU)
Griddle	80,000	8,000
Broiler	75,000	8,250
Range	110,000	8,800
Fryer	240,000	4,800
Other Electric Equipi	122,494	12,249
Total		42,099

Project Equipment List and Load Calculation Example
Marvin Waxman Consulting Engineers

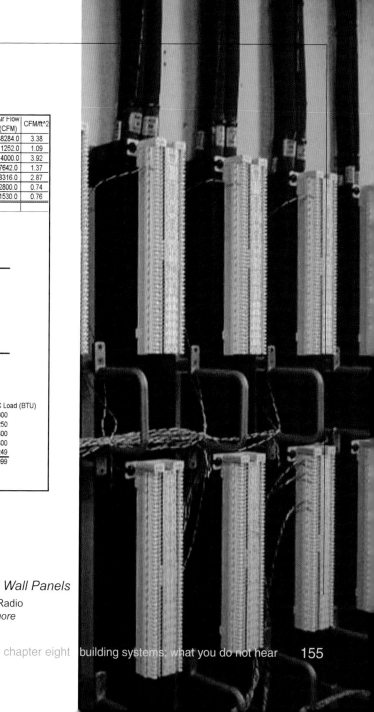

TOC Wall Panels
CBS Radio
Baltimore

The Ultimate Use of Space and Noise Criteria
Close coordination between the acoustic consultant and the mechanical engineer from the project's early stages is implicit in determining the acoustic sensitivity of the station's spaces. For a studio, even a miniscule amount of audible ambient air noise coming from vents may mean that some broadcasting or recording activities can't take place.

Prior to design and documentation, the architect or acoustic consultant will transmit a report to the mechanical engineer. It will give in detail the noise criteria (NC) to be achieved for each space. Criteria are different for studios, open office areas, and private offices, and considers breakout and transmission noise. To satisfy these criteria, the engineer can select from such options as the amount of wrapping specified for ducts, and treatment of diffusers and fans to get appropriate levels of air flow.

Interior spaces (those not on exterior walls) are easier for the engineer to deal with. They represent a controlled atmosphere where the load is consistent and won't change,

so external noise can be eliminated. Citing community relations or station promotion, station management may want to locate a studio on a windowed perimeter of the building. Such variables as external sounds created by wind, rain, and traffic need to be integrated into determining the NC requirements for such areas.

Mechanical VAV Boxes
CBS Radio
Baltimore

Equipment Placement

Some guidelines for location of major HVAC equipment:

- A high-rise building may not offer the option of placing equipment such as chillers or generators on the roof. This information should be provided during the lease negotiation phase; confirm.

- If heavy pieces of equipment have to be installed inside the building, the structural engineer and the architect will be consulted regarding placement and the allowable floor loads.

- Mechanical and electrical equipment (ie. a generator) are typically loud when in operation. The further it is placed away from studios, the better. Placement on the roof, near the loading dock, or in the basement is highly recommended.

Mechanical Equipment in Recessed Areaway
Cox Radio
Orlando

Energy Considerations

Energy usage measurement in watts/sq.ft. for a radio station will be an average of typical and atypical areas. Studios, for example, require more energy to run broadcast and HVAC equipment than typical office areas. Support services that function on a typical five-day workweek cycle can be calculated on usage levels established for offices in high-rise or free-standing structures. Auxiliary spaces that are on a 24/7 schedule (such as a newsroom) need basic services for power and temperature control. The continuity of broadcasting during a power failure involves two sources of power: batteries and generators. Instantaneous switch over is achieved by an uninterrupted power supply (UPS).

These back-up systems should be part of the architect's space allocations. The engineer can prepare a comparison of cost versus the amount of time the generator can be depended upon, and the quality of its performance.

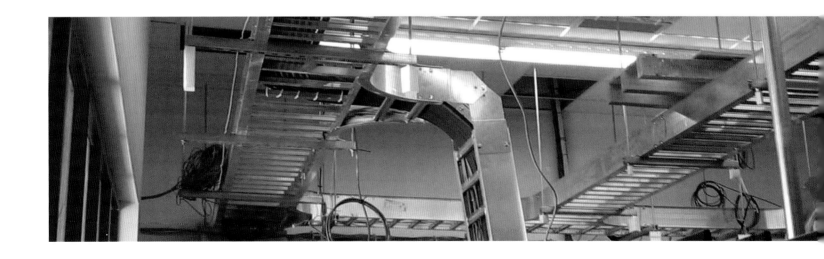

Solving Post-Construction Problems
Accurate installation of equipment in the manner it was designed is, of course, an objective of the entire design team and station management. During the course of construction, the mechanical engineer will monitor the progress of the installation to ascertain if it is in conformance with their documents.

Should acoustic measurements taken after construction reveal an NC level higher than was agreed to, the engineer and the acoustician will examine the installation to determine the cause for the unwanted noise. The two basic sources of cause are design deficiency and/or installation. Either situation is normally correctable with the cooperation of the design and contracting teams.

Throughout the life of the project, the mechanical engineer is always on call to consult on changes, upgrades, and modifications to keep the station operating at full and efficient output.

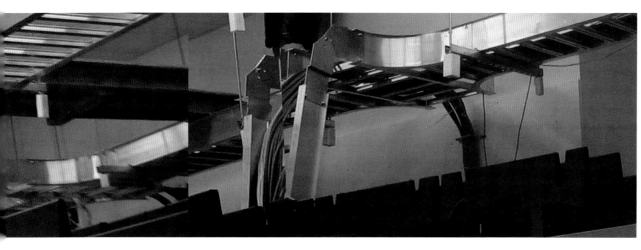

Cable Tray
CBS Radio
Baltimore

Acoustics for Radio Station Facilities

Jim Merrill
Shen Milsom & Wilke, Inc.
Princeton Junction, New Jersey

A radio facility's paramount acoustic environments are the on-air suites, production, edit, and control areas. For these areas, the physical acoustics must be carefully considered and properly planned to produce the most cost-effective acoustic design.

Nearly flawless acoustics are essential to the success of the building program for new or renovated radio stations. The project's acoustic aspects must be addressed at the inception of the program in order to handle the physical, logistic, aesthetic, and marketing constraints that invariably create challenges to the acoustic design and budget.

Air Studio
WHYY
Philadelphia

Space Orientation and Placement

The technical areas of the project require specific acoustic environments to function properly. Locating technical areas away from noise sources and high-circulation areas can help reduce the acoustic considerations, and thus result in more cost-effective solutions. Many designers overlook the potential for noise intrusion from "external" sources in the environment that might be genuinely outside of the building, or that may seep in from directly adjacent spaces.

On-air, production, edit, and control spaces typically require a "quiet" environment with minimal intrusion from external and extraneous sources. It is good design practice to locate these areas away from:

- Mechanical and electrical rooms (base building and tenant)

- External sources such as traffic, train, or aircraft noise

- Highly trafficked circulation corridors

- Loading docks and similar service areas

Noise intrusion levels typically should be controlled within 5 dB (re: 20microPa) within any octave band of the continuous background sound design goal for the space. This typically results in minimal perception of the intruding noise and minimal influence on the outgoing or recorded material. A less stringent limit of 10 dB or slightly more could be considered for less critical areas, or if the budget runs thin.

More noise intrusion is typically tolerable for low frequencies, within or below the 125 Hz octave band. This, however, is not necessarily the case for live or recorded music-oriented spaces where full spectrum sound comes into consideration.

Envelope construction for acoustically critical areas can overcome all but the most extreme adjacencies, but at a cost. The surrounding construction for extreme conditions, and/or for spaces where minimal noise intrusion is desired, involves acoustically decoupled construction (room-within-a-room, discussed later in this section).

Acoustic Separation and Isolation

The surrounding construction, typically partitions and doors, must provide the proper acoustic separation from surrounding noise sources. The "louder" the sources and/or the "quieter" the background sound level within the technical space, the heavier the surrounding construction needs to be. Loud sources, such as those outlined above, would require more construction to isolate the area properly.

Conversely, if the background sound design goal within the critical space is extremely low, more construction will be necessary to ensure intruding sounds are within acceptable limits. On-air and recording spaces are typically the most critical as they have the lowest background sound design goal, and thus require the highest level of acoustic isolation. Locating these spaces in remote areas is ideal from an acoustic standpoint.

Even with careful analysis and engineering design, it is not unusual to find that activities within the station, as well as remote within the same building, can impact the acoustic environment. One example is construction within the same building where demolition and construction activities can easily transmit unwanted noise and vibration.

Acoustically decoupled isolation construction generally consists of a "floating" floor, independent walls on the floating floor, and a resiliently suspended or independent sound barrier ceiling. The entire envelope is resiliently connected to the base building and surrounding construction. Commonly called a "room-within-a-room," there is no direct contact or connection with the surrounding construction.

 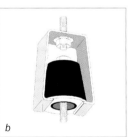 

a   b   c

Isolation Hangers, from:
a. Kinectics
b. Mason
c. Vibration Mounting Controls

Floating Floors

The floor construction is mounted on a material that acoustically decouples it from the base building, typically an engineered isolation device or material similar to rubber, fiberglass, or springs. Walls are normally constructed along the edge of the floating floor and are resiliently braced along the height and at the top. Overhead, the ceiling can be resiliently suspended from above or built with joists from wall to wall. Wall and ceiling weights must be considered within the floating floor isolation selection and spacing.

Floor construction and the isolation material used are dependent on the source(s) of noise to be reduced and the background sound design goal within the critical space. Concrete construction for floors and walls (and in rare cases, ceilings) is typically indicated to isolate loud and low-frequency sound sources. This approach might be implemented to achieve extremely low background sound levels with minimal intrusion.

Otherwise, a cross-section with multi-layer drywall and cement board on studs with insulation between studs can provide significant isolation.

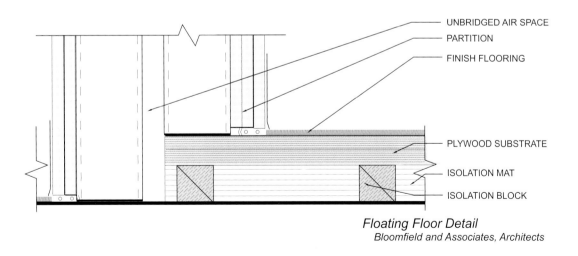

UNBRIDGED AIR SPACE
PARTITION
FINISH FLOORING
PLYWOOD SUBSTRATE
ISOLATION MAT
ISOLATION BLOCK

Floating Floor Detail
Bloomfield and Associates, Architects

Doors

Sound lock vestibules and controlled corridor type layouts are typically ideal approaches for acoustically critical spaces to provide a high degree of acoustic separation. Often, available space limits this option.

An ideal approach is to provide acoustically rated assemblies, which consist of the door leaf, frame, acoustic seals, and hinges. Handle, latch, and closure hardware are added. The closer, if needed, should be on the pull side of the door. (Acoustic seals added to standard or upgraded door leaves typically do not perform well in the installed condition, often as a result of improper installation and field adjustment.) Magnetic head and jamb seals on poly-filled metal doors should be considered since they are self-adjusting. However, acoustically rated assemblies should be seriously considered.

Studio Door
CBS Radio
Baltimore

Windows

Acoustic separation for windows between spaces should be on par with the wall construction requirements. Two panes of thick laminated glass with significant air space between is a common option. Glass is typically angled in order to help improve acoustic separation, but also to control sound reflections within the spaces (as discussed later). Window pane frames are independent when room-within-a-room construction is called for.

High levels of acoustic separation can be provided with upgraded partition construction. Nonetheless, the critical space will always be "exposed" to base building sounds due to the common floor construction. Because sound energy within the common floor can easily flank or transmit across even the best partition construction, acoustically decoupled isolation construction is often a potential solution. The metric for sound separation, in the United States, is Sound Transmission Class (STC).

Acoustic separation for normal construction is limited to the 55-60 range (despite the laboratory tested STC rating of the partition itself). Acoustically decoupled construction provides separation greater than 60, especially where extraneous noise intrusion must be kept to an absolute minimum.

WBBM Studio Window
CBS Radio
Chicago

Background Sound Levels

Background sound is typically controlled by mechanical systems (HVAC) serving the space. The common U.S. metric for background sound are Room Criteria (RC) and Noise Criteria (NC). Each is explained in detail in the latest ASHRAE Handbook.

Room Criteria is an average of three middle frequencies. A "Quality Assessment Index" is applied to the sound spectrum to define whether the sound is "neutral," "rumbly", and/or "hissy". These are good descriptors for the perception of the sound, but not used well as criteria or goals. Noise Criteria defines maximum sound levels within individual

Space	Noise Criteria (NC) Design Goal	Comment
On-Air, Production, Recording Spaces	NC 20-25	Extremely critical environments may want an NC 15-20
Edit, Ingest, Control (w/ no open mics)	NC 25-30	Open mic Control Rooms should be considered On-Air spaces
Executive Offices, High-Profile Conference Rooms	NC 30-35	N/A
General Enclosed Offices and Conference Rooms	NC 35-40	N/A
Open Plan Spaces	NC 40-45	N/A
Rack Technical Equipment Rooms	NC 50-55	N/A

Recommended Standard Design Goals
Shen Milsom & Wilke, Inc.

octave band frequencies, and thus, can be used as a defining criteria or goal. Most air delivery devices have published information that relates to Noise Criteria (NC) levels.

For technical spaces, the appropriate background sound goal depends on the criticality of the listening, recording, and/or broadcast activity. The lower the level, the "quieter" the sound.

The design goal should be the low end of the range, while the upper level could be considered a design tolerance. These levels pertain to the continuous sound level produced by mechanical systems serving the spaces at full air flow conditions.

Where background sound levels are NC 25 or lower, acoustically decoupled (room-within-a-room) construction is indicated in order to limit noise intrusion to within 5-10 dB above the continuous background sound level. (See previous discussion.)

Sound levels 5-10 NC points higher can normally be tolerated for instructional and tutorial type spaces where production quality does not necessarily need to be state-of-the-art, and/or where budget constraints limit certain approaches. In the latter case, the end user group must understand that mechanical noise levels will be quite evident and may have an impact on the quality of the outgoing or recorded signal.

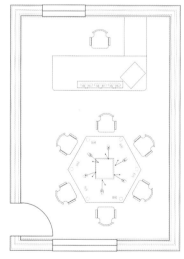

Air Studio
typical wall in plan

Background sound levels of NC 30 or lower require specific design and implementation measures. The general concepts are:

- Place fans and/or air regulation devices remote of the critical area. The distance away depends on the size and type of fan or device. A general rule of thumb for fans is 30-40 feet, and 10-20 feet for air regulation devices (pressure reducing boxes).

- Provide significant in-duct attenuation for fans and air regulation devices. This can be in the form of large plenums, additional distance, acoustic lining (if acceptable for the project), pre-fabricated attenuators, and/or flexible duct work.

- Size duct work for low air velocities to properly control air turbulence-generated noise. The appropriate velocities are dependent on many factors, including duct fittings, acoustic lining, amount of air, distance to occupants, etc.

Noise Criteria (NC) Design Goal	Air Velocity at 0-5 Feet from Air Outlet or Air Inlet (FPM: Feet per Minute)	Comment
NC 20	250 FPM	
NC 25	300 FPM	
NC 30	400 FPM	Or as needed to achieve diffuser or grille acoustical rating.
NC 35	500 FPM	

General Guidelines – Air Velocity FPM to Noise Criteria
Shen Milsom & Wilke, Inc.

General rules of thumb are as follows:

- Provide volume dampers within duct work 5+/- feet from air outlets and inlets in some cases to balance ducted return air. The optimum approach is to design the air distribution duct for equal pressure drop–equal lengths and fittings–for branches to diffusers or grilles. This self-balancing design would not require volume dampers.

- Select diffusers for at least 5 NC points below the room design goal. Perforated and plaque face diffusers should be selected 10 NC points below room design goals. Do not provide equalization grids and/or dampers within diffuser necks or immediately behind grilles.

- Do not place diffusers or grilles within 3+/- feet of microphones.

Background sound levels within many spaces can be controlled by electronic devices within the room, such as small ventilation fans within computers, power supplies, amplifiers, mix boards, etc. Another option is to locate "noisy" equipment outside of the room and/or within enclosed and "quietly" ventilated cabinets. Lighting types, ballasts, and dimming devices must also be considered within the design to limit noise levels within a room.

Studio Window
Entercom Communications
New Orleans

Interior Acoustics

Interior acoustics relates to the way sound propagates within an enclosed space. The properties of a space that dictate the interior acoustics are a strategic combination of sound reflection, diffusion, and absorption.

Listening and High-End Studios

In most cases, the interior acoustics of the critical listening and high-end production/recording rooms are a personal preference and should be coordinated with the primary user or user group. Variable acoustic elements may be considered, such as heavy moveable drapery, diffusive or reflective door faces that expose sound absorption when open, and many other types of approaches and elements.

Room Modes

For on-air radio spaces, sound absorption is the primary consideration. Room modes, or lack thereof, are also an issue. Room modes are sound build-up or focusing due to standing wave reflections. All surfaces above chair rail height, including the ceiling, are best treated with a 2-4-inch thickness of sound absorptive material (fabric-wrapped fiberglass panels). This provides high levels of sound absorption (95-100%) within voice frequencies. Music production spaces require further consideration in terms of low-frequency absorption by use of thicker materials, diffusion, and reflection. The acoustic treatment of music spaces can be personal preference.

The need to control room modes is a function of the dimensions relative to the reflected sound wave. When providing high levels of sound absorption within the frequencies of concern, room modes are typically not a big issue.

However, with limited sound absorption and for music production spaces, room modes must be studied in detail. Angling walls and the ceiling relative to the opposite plane is a typical approach in controlling room modes. Diffusion elements can be installed, although they have limited affect at frequencies lower than the voice spectrum.

Angled walls, windows, and ceiling elements can also help with propagation and reflection of sound within the room. A quick initial reflection can be very important for music and within larger spaces to provide a fullness and spatial sense to the sound and room. However, in radio-oriented spaces, essentially all reflections are to be carefully controlled or avoided. Thick sound absorptive treatment, as previously noted, will do this for the walls.

Hard surfaces, such as doors and windows, should be angled to avoid "bounce-back" of sound directly to the source(s). The angle of windows must be coordinated with lighting and spectral reflections to avoid glare and odd lighting effects, especially for studios that have a television component.

Component	Consideration/Rating
Partial Height Screens	**High Performance Acoustical**
Articulation Class (AC)	170 minimum
Sound absorptive properties	NRC(1) 0.75+
Sound barrier properties	STC(2) 20±
Height	60+ inches
Orientation	Between each workstation 12 feet between workers
Ceiling	**Fiberglass Ceiling Tile w/ backing**
Sound absorptive properties	NRC 0.85+
Configuration	Full coverage
Lighting	Ambient and/or Parabolic lenses
Return Air	No direct openings in ceiling
Background Sound	
Overall level	Noise Criteria (NC) 40
Type of sound (produced by electronic masking sound	Continuous uniform random sound (sounds like diffuser air noise)

(1) Noise Reduction Coefficient (NRC)
(2) Sound Transmission Class (STC)

Major Components to Achieve Subjective Speech Privacy Within an Open Office Environment
Shen Milsom & Wilke, Inc.

Open Plan Office Spaces

Layouts based on the open office concept or its variations, such as partial-height screen offices, are meant to promote interaction and communication between personnel. A rating of "Fair" to "Good" voice privacy is achievable in an open plan environment by:

- Reducing the sound between workstations along the direct path, taking into consideration the furniture system and the ceiling's physical/acoustic properties.

- Providing a continuous background sound within the area using a masking sound system.

With these techniques, normal voice levels in the adjacent workstation will be audible but unintelligible most of the time. Raised voices and speakerphones are intelligible.

Open Office Speech Privacy Components

Most open plan areas do not require the degree of optimum speech privacy indicated. Where privacy is a concern, such as for conference rooms and director's offices, full-height (to structure) partitions with insulation should be provided. Multiple layer drywall partitions with insulation can be considered for high-level executive and conference rooms and presentation-type spaces.

If masking sound is required, the cost can be in the low $1.00/sq.ft. range for a standard masking system. Three-dimensional solutions, such as high-performance office screens and ceiling tiles, represent moderate premiums over standard products.

End-users are the best source of information to the design team to convey their individual preferences for privacy within the open plan.

Preliminary Open Office Rendering
Entercom Communications
Kansas City

Design and Photo Credits

Mechanical and Acoustic Resources

− Manufacturers of Back-Up Generators
  - Kohler (www.kohler.com/hub/powersystem.html)
  - Ransom
  - Cummins

− Manufacturers of HVAC Equipment (Data Controls)
  - Leibert (www.liebert.com)
  - Data-Aire Inc. (www.dataaire.com)
  - Stoltz

− Manufacturers of UPS
  - IBM (www.IBM.com)
  - Falcon Electric Inc. (www.falconups.com)
  - APC - American Power Conversion (www.apc.com)

− Manufacturers of *room-within-a-room* isolation devices and materials:
  - Mason Industries (www.mason-ind.com)
  - Kinetics Noise Control (www.kineticsnoise.com)
  - Vibration Mountings & Controls (www.vmc-kdc.com)

− Acoustic door and window manufacturers:
  - Industrial Acoustics Company (www.industrialacoustics.com)
  - Overly Manufacturing Company (www.overly.com)
  - Kreiger (www.kriegerproducts.com)

Acoustic Consultant Checklist

A professional who specializes in acoustic performance and design approaches will focus on these project aspects:

− Evaluate proposed areas for acoustically critical spaces: on-air, production, edit, etc.

− Establish acoustic design criteria.

− Recommend construction and provide details for proper acoustic separation.

− Recommend mechanical, electrical, and conveying system noise and vibration control.

− Recommend size, shape and finishes for acoustic response.

− Review drawings and specifications for proper inclusion of acoustic considerations and recommendations.

− Review shop drawings and submittals pertaining to acoustic design issues for compliance with design intent and contract documents.

− Conduct site visits to ensure proper implementation of acoustic construction and conditions. Also review field conditions for modifications to design approach if necessary.

− Conduct testing to ensure compliance with acoustic goals and design intent.

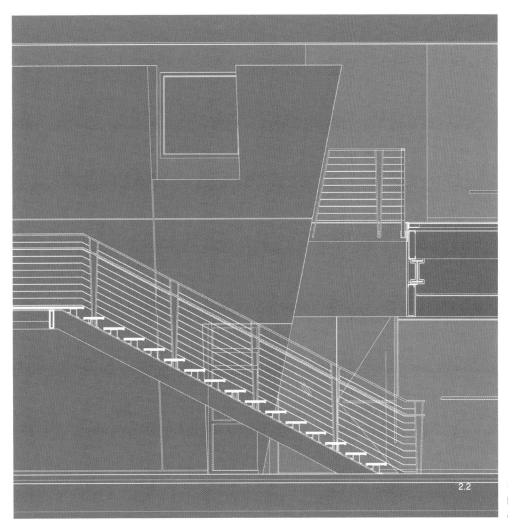

2.2

Stair Detail

Entercom Communications
Denver

chapter nine

bidding and procurement: buying the construction services

This chapter will present an overview of procurement options and introduce terms that you most likely will encounter during the bidding process.

Once the station's goals have been determined, the design completed, and construction documents exacted, the project team will expand, including those who will actually pound the nails in and paint the walls: the contractor and subcontractors.

General guidelines to assist in contractor selection are explained, as well as how the relationships of time, quality, and cost are structured within the various procurement methods.

The selection of a contractor will be one of the most important decisions to be made. It will have a direct impact on the success of the project. The input and recommendations from all team members should be carefully considered.

All procurement methods assign responsibility; who is going to do what, what is going to be accomplished, when will it be completed, and how much will it cost. Today, with the reshuffling of roles and responsibilities, new procurement methods are being developed in response to market demands.

It is common during the feasibility planning and design stages to have design team members assist in evaluating procurement options. Integral to the process is the selection of contractors with proven success on projects of similar scale and type.

There are three basic procurement methods available and the goal is to dovetail contractor experience and procurement method with your project.

The basic procurement methods are:

- Traditional Bid
- Negotiated Fee
- Design Build

Construction Photo
Entercom Communications
Denver

Traditional Bid

This method of procurement invites contractors, who are typically pre-approved, to bid on a defined scope of work. The contractors review bid documents and submit associated costs in the form of a bid to perform the work. Bid documents typically consist of drawings, specifications, and a project schedule. Together, they establish the basis for expectations and a means for quality control. The bid process also allows your team to define the time frame within which the work is to be completed and establish ercussions for failure to meet deadlines.

The competive bid structure is a time-proven method for both public and private works. Cost benefits are achieved through the competitive bidding situation, and responds to what the market will bear. The bids and accompanying qualifications should be carefully reviewed. The lowest bid may not be the most appropriate.

The architect will create a specialized bid form to assure ease of comparison. When compared with other procurement methods, this type can

Main Studio Core
Entercom Communications
Denver

protract the start of construction. The traditional bid process has evolved over the course of time into two basic types: **Open Bid** and **Closed Bid**.

Open Bid

The Open Bid process is traditionally used for public works as it proclaims equality towards bidders and in theory, the best use of public funds. This process is the most competitive, as there is a larger pool of contractors to draw upon. The review of all bids requires a significant amount of time.

Closed Bid

The Closed Bid process has been developed to reduce time associated with an Open Bid. It is a cost-effective option for procuring private works. The idea is to pre-qualify a limited pool of proven contractors while capitalizing on the cost benefits that a competitive bid situation offers.

Bid Documents

The package of information released to

Lobby Session Studio
Entercom Communications
Under Construction
Greenville

contractors for competitive bidding is known as "bid documents," or the "bidding package." Regardless of the procurement method employed, this information at one point or another will be prepared by the design team, released to the contractors, and used to establish contractual terms and conditions by which the work is to be performed.

The documents consist of:

- A bid form outlining terms and conditions.

- A bid tabulation form indicating the schedule of values for work to be performed.

- Drawings and specification describing design intent for all aspects of construction.

Lobby Session Studio
Entercom Communications
Construction Completed
Greenville

Negotiated Fee

This method of procurement selects a general contractor or construction manager during the design process and before a complete scope of work is established. With this approach, the relationships between time, quality, and costs can be targeted towards specific goals.

One scenario is that you already have a good working relationship with a general contractor and there is no reason to look any further. In this case, the quality of the finished product and the time benefits of utilizing a known quantity out-weigh potential cost savings.

Another scenario is to pre-select a general contractor during the design process utilizing, their pricing, scheduling, and management services to inform the design process. If the project is time-driven, and the goal is to reduce the overall construction period, efforts can be directed to identify scopes of work that can be quantified and performed early on.

If the project is cost-driven, efforts can be directed to secure competitive bid pricing from multiple subcontractors under the control of the General Contractor. Identify measures that will cut costs by capitalizing on available materials and construction methods. Regardless of the scenario, this procurement method will remain an open-ended process until the scope of work is defined, the final schedule confirmed, and quality expectation levels agreed upon.

When employing the Negotiated Fee method, the selection of one contractor over another is usually based upon related experience and associated fees. Care should be taken to find a contractor with a proven success on projects of similar scale and scope.

One category of costs is General Conditions. These include expenses for the management, job superintendent, building permits, temporary utilities, job site accommodations and other required items to actualize the project.

Overhead and Profit is another category and is commonly identified as a percentage of construction. This is the markup a contractor adds on to their subcontractors as well as materials and services they directly provide. All of these fees should be carefully reviewed by key team members for omissions, redundancies, and reasonableness.

The Negotiated Fee procurement method can involve two distinct processes: Guaranteed Maximum Price and Cost Plus.

GMP (Guaranteed Maximum Price)
This process establishes a fixed price based upon a partially defined scope of work. The goal is early budget confirmation, and associated time reductions. This is achieved by locking into a Guaranteed Maximum Price based upon 75 percent to 90 percent complete drawings and specifications. It eliminates time associated with the bidding process, allowing for early commencement of construction without a 100 percent complete set of bidding documents.

Foundation Under Construction
Cox Radio
Orlando

While this GMP is a proven procurement method for development projects, the unique aspects of a broadcast facility can disrupt the process. Specifically, the design and specifications for studio assemblies completed during the last 10 percent to 25 percent of the design process, are a potential stumbling block.

It is important to keep in mind that with this GMP structure, the overhead and profit amounts are established for the contractor. When there are oversights or errors during construction, it is not uncommon for the general contractor to request or make substitutions at the end of a project to maintain the guaranteed price.

Cost Plus

This process establishes up-front fees that a general contractor will charge for overhead and profit. These are typically identified as a percentage of construction. Total cost to the owner is the sum of all costs incurred by the general contractor plus an agreed-upon fixed fee as a percentage of work performed. The principal difference between GMP and Cost Plus is that with the "Cost Plus" method the final price is not fixed until the scope of work is defined.

Cost benefits are attained through early general contractor involvement by competitively bidding discrete packages. This will serve to establish budget conformity and capitalize on available materials and construction methods.

The overall project period is reduced by eliminating the bidding phase so the work can commence without complete drawings and specifications. Unique to this process is the ability to establish and maintain consistent quality levels and associated expectations from the beginning of the project.

Design Build

With the higher construction quality demands now in place in Europe and Asia, the Design Build model is becoming the delivery and procurement method of choice. Here, the collaborative efforts between architectural, engineering, and construction disciplines have blurred distinctions and erased traditional boundaries to form a new typology that is single-sources responsibility.

In the European context, the utilization of lean project management objectives has in some cases, attained a higher quality end product, delivered in a shortened time period at reduced costs. In North America, Design Build models are evolving in response to this model. One approach is to assemble a Design Build team that includes experienced independent architectural, engineering, and construction professionals into a joint venture contractual relationship this method typically works best on large scale projects.

Within the past few years, this model has successfully delivered complex industrial and chemical processing facilities and is becoming an effective model for civil infrastructure projects. It may only be a matter of time before this method becomes a viable alternative for delivering a broadcast facility.

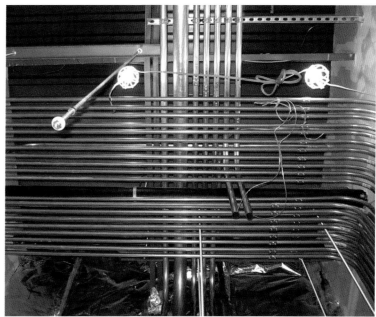

Electrical Conduit
Entercom Communication
New Orleans

Design and Photo Credits

p 176   Stair Detail
Entercom Communications
Denver, Colorado
Source: Bloomfield & Associates, Architects

p 178   Construction Photo
Entercom Communications
Denver, Colorado
Source: Bloomfield & Associates, Architects

p 179   Main Studio Core
Entercom Communications
Denver, Colorado
Source: Bloomfield & Associates, Architects

p 180   Lobby Session Studio – Under Construction
Entercom Communications
Greenville, South Carolina
Source: Bloomfield & Associates, Architects

p 181   Lobby Session Studio – Construction Complete
Entercom Communications
Greenville, South Carolina
Source: Bloomfield & Associates, Architects

p 183   Foundation Under Construction
Cox Radio
Orlando, Florida
Source: Bloomfield & Associates, Architects

p 185   Electrical Conduit
Entercom Communications
New Orleans, Louisiana
Source: Bloomfield & Associates, Architects

Procurement Checklist

– Establish optimal procurement method

– Review contractor qualifications

– Review and verify contractor references

– Visit examples of contractor's work

– Assemble bid / procurement documents:
  - Drawings and specifications
  - Project schedule
  - Copy of pertinent AIA contract
  - Secure waiver of liens (where applicable)
  - Secure bid / performance bonding requirements (when required)
  - Confirm landlord fit-out requirements (where applicable)
  - Instruction to bidders
  - Bid form
  - Bid tabulation form
  - Bid alternates
  - Bid allowances
  - Bid addenda

– Establish and delegate bid review tasks.

Entry
Chancellor Media
Philadelphia

chapter ten

case studies

The goal of assembling the following case studies is to illustrate a variety of domains and diverse user needs. They are a cross-section of urban and rural, new construction and renovation, academic and corporate, single tenant or multi-tenant facility.

All of these projects are working facilities that started with a series of ideas that were then incorporated into the normal limitations and opportunities associated with every site.

Ultimately, because it is the organizational scheme that will determine how the facility functions on a day-to-day basis, we have included plans and other drawings wherever possible. In that way we are able to show how the three-dimensional reality was translated from two-dimensional concepts.

Renovation of an Independent Building in a Suburban Context

Entercom Communications
Greenville, South Carolina
Bloomfield & Associates, Architects

Project Scope: A newly occupied building to accommodate and reorganize a five-station group.

Additional Features:
- Re-design of an existing two-story facility.
- Exterior renovations (facade and entry).
- New outdoor performance space.

The 25,000-sq.-ft. building, located on a busy thoroughfare in Greenville, is visible from the intersection of two major state highways, routes 85 and 385.

One of the most challenging aspects of this project was the extensive redesign of the complex engineering system. Accordingly, the architects worked closely with the station's Director of Engineering to integrate both the technology and controls of the station into the new space. Square footage was maximized and convenient accessibility to the building was maintained.

A new color palette was selected and incorporates the colors of individual station logos as background and accent tones.

To emphasize its ties to the local market, Entercom commissioned the design and construction of an outdoor performance space to be used for concerts, radio promotions, and various community events.

Existing Building

New Facility: Main Entry Renovation

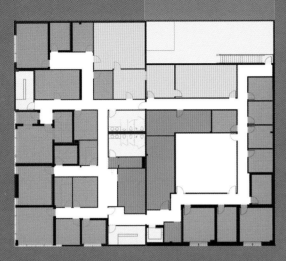

2nd Floor Plan

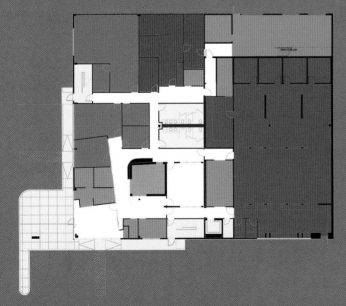

1st Floor Plan

Session Studio in Lobby

Key

■ Administrative
■ Sales/Development
▨ Engineering
▨ Studios/Prod.
■ Promotions
▨ Support
▢ Common

Main Lobby

TOC Engineering Room

Exterior Detail

Renovation of Tenant Facility in a Downtown Center

Cox Radio
Birmingham, Alabama
Bloomfield & Associates, Architects

Project Scope: A new facility to accommodate an expanding work force, and establish a strong downtown presence.

As the leader in Birmingham's urban broadcasting, the decision to remain downtown was clear.

Management perceived their station cluster as one entity working together for the success of the greater community. This guided the analysis of three potential sites, taking into consideration the following categories:

- Initial cost of renovation.
- Operating costs over the life of the lease (annual rental rate, utility costs, parking, cleaning, etc.).
- General location suitability.
- Ability of existing conditions to satisfy current and projected technology requirements.
- Engineering opportunities and constraints.

The site selection criteria was satisfied with a 16,000-sq.-ft. space on the tenth floor of the Medical Forum Building, a downtown office building owned by the City. Located in the Birmingham Convention Center, it offered an aggressive rent deal, easily addressed engineering issues, and provided a location appropriate for Cox's vision of their urban stations.

The broadcast facility is envisioned as an additional component of the Civic Center which also includes a major hotel with meeting rooms, auditoriums, restaurants, etc. Other tenants include ad agencies, communications companies, and professional offices.

Reception Lobby

Floor Plan

Cox Radio
Birmingham, Alabama
Bloomfield & Associates, Architects

Views on three sides are of downtown and the city's periphery. There is easy access to the roof which is located directly above; its full use was offered by the landlord as part of base lease terms. From the roof, there is a direct sight-line to the tower aiding in engineering efficiency.

The landlord also facilitated the installation of a back-up generator which is located in the parking garage below.

The design process, from start of demolition to the completion of finishes, was accomplished in eight months, permitting the client to move in to their facility on schedule.

Key
■ Administrative
■ Sales/Development
▦ Engineering
■ Studios/Prod.
■ Promotions
■ Support
□ Common

Central Hall

Air Studio

Common Area

Break Room

Fit-Out of a Tenant Facility in an Urban Context
WRTI
Philadelphia, Pennsylvania
Burt Hill, Architecture and Engineering

Project Scope: A new facility to accommodate expanded operations of a university sponsored radio station.

Additional Features:
- This facility houses state-of-the-art production and broadcasting equipment, and new office space for support personnel.
- The plan includes flexible facilities so the station could offer activities to widen its services for listeners.

Licensed by Temple University, WRTI has grown to become the highest-rated, all-music NPR (National Public Radio) station in the country. It offers classical music during the day, and jazz in the evening and through the night. Temple's main campus is in North Philadelphia, with other specialty colleges and divisions located around the Philadelphia region. WRTI identifies itself as the NPR voice of the university and the surrounding community.

The station occupied a 2,300-sq.-ft. office suite, but the station had long ago outgrown the space. With funding from both the University and WRTI's donors, the station relocated its headquarters to a newly constructed building at Fifteenth Street and Cecil B. Moore Avenue.

Main Conference Room

Upon entering the station's headquarters, the interior workings of the broadcast facility are immediately visible. The on-air master control studio with a large glass window can be viewed inside a frame of burnished metal.

The station contains six production studios, a live performance studio with recording capabilities, two internal edit booths, and a news production room.

Reception

Entry View to Air Studio

New Construction of an Independent Building in a Downtown Center
WHYY
Philadelphia, Pennsylvania
Burt Hill, Architecture and Engineering

Project Scope: A new building to create an image for public radio and television.

Additional Features:
- The stand-alone structure is a recognizable downtown media landmark.
- This project reinforces the image of accessibility by the public and its stature in the community.

Located in the historic Independence Mall area in downtown Philadelphia, the public broadcasting station WHYY is an example of success that can also be applied by other public radio stations. With its dramatically illuminated front façade, it is a broadcasting landmark that showcases the interior of the building's ground-level studios and offices above.

The façade was conceived by the architects as a giant screen in a transparent glass skin that translates the internal broadcast media into a changing panorama. The personalities and activities of WHYY FM and WHYY TV12, plus community events held in the building, are in full view of the public.

Common Area

Exterior View

WHYY currently occupies 70,000 square feet of space in Center City Philadelphia, and has made its educational mission more dynamic by branching out of the traditional media format.

This shift required the complete replacement of the station's existing facility and an addition of new auxiliary space.

Production Studio

Air Studio

Main Entry Railing Detail

Common Area

Fit-Out of a Tennant Facility in a Suburban Context

CBS Radio
Baltimore, Maryland
Bloomfield & Associates, Architects

Project Scope: A new facility to house and consolidate five fully functional radio stations.

Additional Features:
- The stations largely function independently but are clustered to share some components.
- Studios were sized to allow for comfort and efficiency.
- The new facility was envisioned as a tool for sales and production.

After fifteen years in a traditional multi-tenant suburban office building located in downtown Towson, Maryland, CBS used the opportunity of a new site to solve some serious concerns.

- Broadcast engineering was difficult in a building with low ceiling heights.
- The aging mechanical system prevented an uncomfortable work environment.
- The building floor plan, which forced CBS to occupy three different floors, hindered team building and operations.
- Employee and visitor parking was both difficult and expensive.

Affordable flexible office space, which provides unobstructed floor area, plenty of parking, and high ceilings, is typically not available in thriving downtown areas. And while the office park setting lacked many of the semi-urban amenities of Towson, the choice was clear. Here was a chance to locate all 30,000-sq-ft. on one floor and organize it in a manner that suited and supported the business plan that management envisioned.

Nine-to-five utilities for the office space were easily accommodated on the roof, as were the specialty 24/7 studio and tech center needs. The high ceilings, along with exposed cabling, afforded a highly organized communications system that became part of the image. The goal was to make both visitors and staff feel like they were entering into a machine for the making of radio. This facility is "broadcasting" that idea far and wide.

Circulation Core

Floor Plan

CBS Radio
Baltimore, Maryland
Bloomfield & Associates, Architects

Main Conference Room

Key
- Administrative
- Sales/Development
- Engineering
- Studios/Prod.
- Promotions
- Support
- Common

Air Studio

Main Corridor Detail

Open Office Space

New Construction of an Independent Building on an Academic Campus

KPLU at Pacific Lutheran University
Tacoma, Washington
Bloomfield & Associates, Architects

Project Scope: The design of a new 24,000-sq.-ft. educational and broadcast facility shared by the University's communications department and nationally recognized NPR jazz station KPLU.

Additional Features:
- The building creates a new entry point and campus landmark.
- It includes an extensive music library open to the public.
- The technologically intensive program includes university meeting spaces, classrooms, and offices.
- The building is to be LEED certified.

KPLU, a National Public Radio affiliate in the State of Washington, has a national reputation for its jazz programming. It is as the national depository for jazz.

The proposed facility, while primarily dedicated to the needs of KPLU, is on the western edge of the Pacific Lutheran University campus and, accordingly, needs to address other academic buildings in an appropriate manner.

The plan is simple, affordable, and time-tested. Support pieces such as stairs, elevator, toilets, etc. are separated from the main body of the building. The result is open space that is easily planned to accommodate both public and university needs as well as specific KPLU requirements.

The building essentially places all the programming and production components on the first floor. Management, support, accounting, traffic, and contributor relations are on the second. The third floor will provide academic services and classrooms. In an effort to fully sequester the broadcast component, the studios will be located in a one-story piece on the front, offering some limited views from the street.

Members of the radio station's community of listeners will see physical evidence of their contributions at work and the building is integral to the fund-raising process.

Exterior Rendering

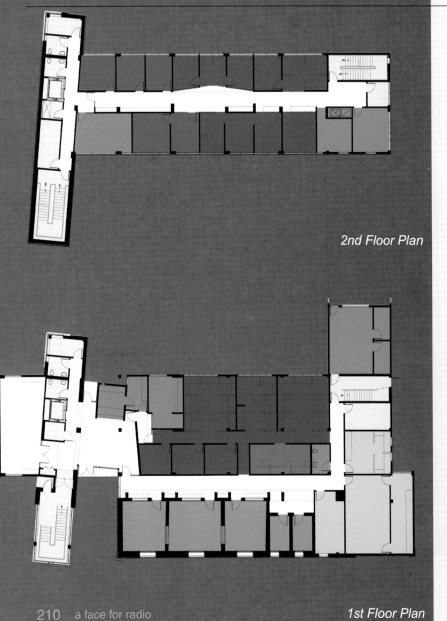

2nd Floor Plan

1st Floor Plan

Key
- Administrative
- Sales/Development
- Engineering
- Studios/Prod.
- Promotions
- Support
- Common

KPLU at Pacific Lutheran University
Tacoma, Washington
Bloomfield & Associates, Architects

Early Concept Watercolors

Rendering of Main Entry

Fit-Out in a Tenant Facility in a Suburban Context

Infinity Broadcasting
Bala Cynwyd, Pennsylvania
Partridge Architects Inc.

Project Scope: A new facility housing three radio stations on two floors of an existing building.

Additional Features:
- The design needed to accommodate groups with very distinct needs—three radio stations, station support, and sales, without compromising either the security or the design of the space.
- Unobtrusive secured control points to manage flow provide the needed security and allow the space to flow consistently.

For three Infinity Broadcasting stations---WOGL, WPHT, and WIP–located in a multi-tenant office building in Bala Cynwyd, a close-in suburb of Philadelphia, a 28,000-sq.-ft. facility was designed to provide:

- private offices
- workstations
- reception area
- conference rooms
- lunchroom; rest rooms
- 8 studios
- 2 production rooms
- 3 edit booths
- technical operations center

Sports talk radio 610/WIP is located on the seventh floor in 10,000-sq.-ft. On the eighth floor in 18,000-sq.-ft. space are WOGL (local oldies) and WPHT (nationally syndicated talk radio). The design challenge was to give each radio station its own distinct identity.

To reinforce 610/WIP's legacy as the station for sports coverage, common areas feature team colors and historic jerseys from three generations of Philadelphia sports teams—the Phillies, Sixers, Eagles and Flyers—punctuated by authentic stadium seating from the now-demolished Veteran's Stadium. Bright accent colors were used for walls, including lime green and yellow. Aluminum, maple, and acrylic panels were coordinated into the final scheme.

The WOGL/WPHT space is organized along two axes. The longitudinal axis separates each station, while a cross axis separates the office side from the operational side. To reflect the very different personalities of WOGL and WPHT, a rich saturated color palette was selected.

Lobby
WOGL / WPHT

Reception
610 / WIP

Accent colors include aubergine, charcoal gray, lipstick red, gold, and chartreuse. Dark wood and industrial-style finishes were used in each station's studios to further differentiate between the two stations sharing the same floor and common areas. Materials that were incorporated into the design include aluminum; metal mesh, mahogany, acrylic panels, and architectural glass.

Illumination in coves at the reception area provides dramatic highlights for the exposed concrete ceiling. MR16 pin spots highlight art walls and metal mesh screens.

Conference Room
WOGL / WPHT

Receptionist Desk
WOGL / WPHT

Shared functions–reception, conference rooms, lunchroom–were placed at the cross sections.

Exacting engineering and acoustic requirements were required for the state-of-the-art studio suites and control rooms. The Technical Operations Center (TOC) features a Tate raised-access flooring system that allows all cables and wiring to run beneath the floor from the TOC to the studios. It holds nine fully loaded racks connected via conduits to satellites on the roof and to the loading dock for cable truck connection for remote broadcasts. The rack room and all studios operate on 24/7 supplemental AC units with UPS system and 100kw backup generator.

Air Studio
WOGL / WPHT

Technical Operations Center
WOGL / WPHT

Addition/Renovation of an Independent Building in a Suburban Context

Clear Channel Communications
Indianapolis, Indiana
Luckett & Farley, Architects & Engineers

Project Scope: Facility renovation and expansion to provide an efficient and functional environment for administrative, sales, production, and broadcast personnel for AM and FM clusters.

Additional Features:

- New construction and renovation of the existing structures accounted for a total of 20,000 sq. ft.
- The site, which is on a flood plain, is also the tower site.
- Portions of the existing building had to remain occupied and operational 24/7 throughout construction.

The design of the new building required construction to be above the flood plain. Architecture and landscaping were integrated into the design program to provide special access needed for an elevated building. Siting around the tower's buried radial grounding system was a second major determinant for the new addition.

An existing water well supply was discontinued, and new water service and utility extension were installed. A new sewage ejector lift station replaced the equipment that was in operation when the upgrading of the original structure began.

To keep the station operational during the construction period, special procedures and requirements were implemented to maintain water, sewer, and electrical services. Whenever possible during weekends and evenings, when the staff was at minimal capacity, construction was scheduled to minimize impact on station employees' work patterns.

One of the features for the interior is a suite for the popular "Bob and Tom Morning Show" including offices, green room, and a performance studio. With its sleek new exterior façade, the building now presents a strong contemporary

Air Studio

Air Studio

Control Room

Lobby / Reception

Main Entry

Renovation of an Independent Building in a Suburban Context

Clear Channel Communications
Little Rock, Arkansas
Luckett & Farley, Architects

Project Scope: Renovations of A 106,000-sq.-ft. former Sam's Club warehouse to house eight radio stations and a TV station.

Additional Features:
- Clear Channel Communications bought the property that contained a vacant Sam's Club distribution center.
- The exterior was re-skinned and windows and skylights added.
- A 20,000-sq.-ft. Events Center is now a profit center.

Management of Clear Channel Communications in Little Rock was initially skeptical that a former warehouse could be made into a pleasant and functioning place to work for all 250 radio and TV station employees. The architects chose not to deny the structure's former industrial use, but to introduce interior daylighting and utilize a sculptural approach to the exterior.

The building's outside metal skin was left intact and recovered. The new façade combines a split face block system up to a 10-ft. height, with exterior-finish gypsum board extending several feet above to the roof line. Around the entrance is a metal open-work arch that resembles the on-site tower's structural frame.

Sales representatives occupy an open bullpen-type space when they are in the office. Because there were no windows or other openings to the outside when the building was a repository for merchandise, large skylights were installed to bring daylight into the station's interior. A bold color scheme combining bright purples and reds enlivens the environment for the sales staff.

Existing Building

New Entry Canopy

A 20,000-sq.-ft. Events Center makes profitable use of extra space within the single-story structure. A full-time staff aggressively promotes the Center's availability for exhibits, community meetings, education, and entertainment activities. Spot announcements are broadcast for these bookings on group stations headquartered at the site.

Energy efficiency technology is employed to minimize operational costs. HVAC equipment is linked to an energy management system. Lighting controls, including lighting sensors, are programmed to direct the illumination level throughout the various work spaces on a 24/7 basis.

Entry Canopy Detail

Air Studio

Reception

Fit-Out of a Tenant Facility in a Suburban Context

Clear Channel Communications
Bala Cynwyd, Pennsylvania
Luckett & Farley, Architects & Engineers

Project Scope: A new facility to house and consolidate a multi-station radio group and entertainment division.

Additional Features:
- Management's goal was to consolidate stations then located at different sites in a single facility.
- Landlord had completed demolition of space that was previously occupied by another firm.
- Special acoustics were required.

With leases expiring at several of its stations that comprise its Philadelphia cluster, plus the obvious benefits of more efficient management, Clear Channel Communications' solution was a single facility located close to the city, highways, and public transportation. The entertainment division was also to be located in the new facility.

Management commissioned comparative financial studies and schematic floor plans of three short-listed sites to judge the fit of the spaces to the programmatic requirements and at the cost to build and operate them. The final nod was given to a site that had already been cleared by the owner, located on the Bala Cynwd side of City Line Avenue, which separates Philadelphia from its western communities.

To make maximum use of the location, the building was sited parallel to the road. Studios placed on the side of the building facing the roadway have special acoustical properties and exterior wall treatments to maintain the interior noise level at studio broadcast quality.

Air Studio

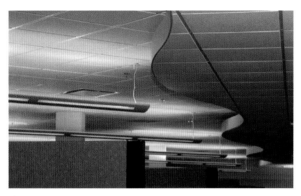

Ceiling Detail

Clear Channel Communications
Bala Cynwyd, Pennsylvania
Luckett & Farley, Architects & Engineers

Interior spaces were designed in a modern design theme, reflecting the upbeat urban quality of its programming. A multi-purpose room fitted with audio/visual, lighting, and sound controls handles meetings, conferences, and training programs.

Special events and guest appearances take place in the facility's performance studio. A fast-track schedule met the six-month timetable from start of construction to move-in.

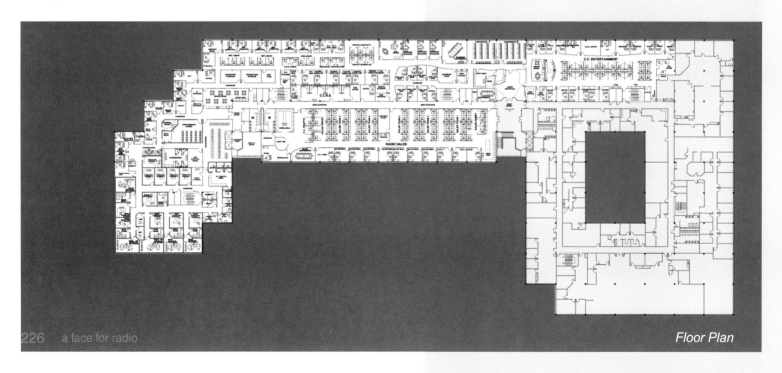

Floor Plan

Open Office Corridor

Meeting Area

Green Room

Reception

Lobby

Renovation of an Independent Building in a Suburban Context.

Clear Channel Communications
Tulsa, Oklahoma
Luckett & Farley, Architects & Engineers

Project Scope: Renovation of an existing building to house 6 radio stations (4 FM, 2 AM) and 2 TV stations.

Additional Features:
- Site is next to a strip mall in a residential neighborhood close to an interstate exit.
- Former 125,000-sq.-ft. Burlington Coat Factory "big box" store was vacant.
- 260-ft.-high tower is on the site.

Clear Channel Communications purchased the parcel of land which contained an operating strip mall plus an empty building which had been a typical concrete "big box" format store occupied by a Burlington Coat Factory unit. The exterior was reconfigured with new fenestration and façade materials that coordinate with the design of the landscaping for a pleasingly balanced environmental effect.

Existing Building

View of Renovation and New Entry Piece

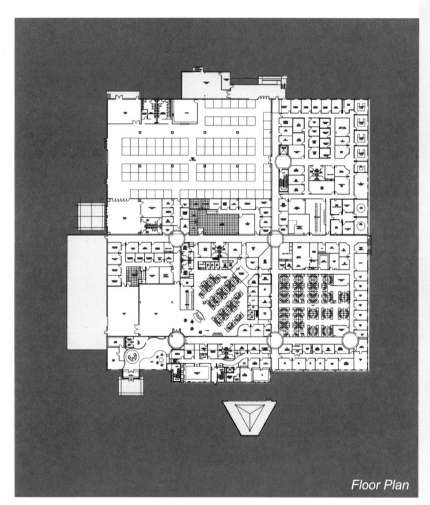

Floor Plan

With residential buildings directly across the street from Clear Channel's proposed headquarters, the station's managers and architect worked with the local community to present plans that would gain zoning approval for the tower. The successful design offered a 30-ft.-high illuminated translucent panel surrounding the tower's base that creates a visual link to the firm's nearby office and studio building.

As is the case with the Clear Channel Little Rock facility, the Tulsa station had excess space that has been turned into a 20,000-sq.-ft. Event Center. It has its own separate entrance, a full-time director, and the infrastructure to host exhibits and conventions as well as a broad spectrum of social and business events. It is also a source of non-traditional revenue and return-on-investment for the broadcast organization.

A new roof was installed to support over a dozen TV satellite dishes. Clear Channel worked with vendors in the adjoining strip mall to update signage and exterior lighting.

Main Lobby

Design and Photo Credits

Main Lobby Rendering
Entercom Communications
Kansas City, Kansas
Bloomfield & Associates, Architects

Amplification
The strengthening of a signal or current without otherwise changing its characteristics.

Audio
Of or pertaining to audible sound, or its broadcasting, or recording and reproduction.

Baffle
A single opaque or translucent element to shield a light source from direct view at certain angles or to absorb unwanted light or sound.

Bid Documents
The completed drawing and specifications needed to assure accurate pricing. Also, the bid form, and the proposed contract documents including any addenda issued prior to the receipt of bids.

Bidding
An offer to perform the work described in a contract at a specified cost.

Broadcasting
A radio communication service of transmissions intended to be received directly by the general public. This service may include transmissions of sounds-radio broadcasting-or transmissions by television, facsimile, or other means. Broadcasting-to everyone-should be distinguished from two-way or point-to-point communication, which was called "narrow casting" in the early 1920s. Narrow casting now refers to the programmer's focus on a specific audience rather than on the public as a whole or on a technical bandwidth limitation.

Building Program
A statement prepared by or for an owner, setting forth the conditions and objectives for a building project, including its general purpose and detailed requirements, such as a complete listing of the rooms required, their sizes, special facilities, etc.

Call Letters
Combinations of letters and sometimes numbers used to identify radio stations over the air. Blocks of initial letters are assigned to a particular country, a practice started as a result of the London International Radiotelegraph Conference of 1912. The United States has been assigned all of the blocks with initial letters W, K, and N, and much of A, although both A and N calls tend to be used mostly by the armed forces. In broadcasting, W is generally used east of the Mississippi and K west, with a few exceptions-usually older stations such as KYW, Philadelphia, and KDKA, Pittsburgh.

Capital Expenditures
Expenditures of money, generally on what are termed fixed assets, i.e., tangibles such as land, buildings, equipment, fixtures, furniture, etc. A characteristic of capital expenditures is that their benefits often accrue in the future.

Color Temperature
The color appearance of various light sources, defined in terms of color temperature, measured in Degrees Kelvin (K). The range is from 1500 for a candle to 9000 for a northlight blue sky.

Concrete frame construction
A structure consisting of concrete beams, girders, and columns which are rigidly joined.

Condenser
A heat-exchange device in a refrigeration system; consisting of a vessel or arrangement of pipes or tubing in which refrigerant vapor is liquefied (condensed) by the removal of heat.

Construction Administration (also Contract Administration)
The duties of the architect during the construction phase.

Construction Cost
The cost of all the construction portions of a project, generally based upon the sum of the construction contrast(s) and other direct construction costs; does not include the compensation paid to the architect and consultants, the cost of the land, tight-of-way, or the other costs which are defined in the contract documents as being the responsibility if the owner.

Construction Documents (working drawings and specifications)
Drawings, intended for use by a contractor, subcontractors, and fabricators, which form part of the contract documents for a building project. They contain the necessary information to manufacture or erect an object or structure. Also, a part of the contract documents contained in the project manual consisting of written descriptions of a technical nature of materials, equipment construction systems, standards, and workmanship.

Construction Documents Phase
The third phase of the architect's basic services. In this phase the architect prepares from the approved design development documents, for approval by the owner, the working drawings and specifications and the necessary bidding information. The architect also assists the owner in the preparation of bidding forms, the conditions of the contract, and the form of agreement between the owner and the contractor.

Construction Management
Management services performed by the architect or others during the construction phase of the project, under separate or special agreement with the owner. This is not part of the architect's basic services, but is an additional service sometimes included in comprehensive services.

Contract Administration
(see Construction Administration)

Contract Documents
Those documents that comprise a contract, e.g., in a construction contract, the owner-contractor agreement, conditions of the contract (generally supplementary, and other conditions), plans and/or drawings, specifications, all addenda, modifications, and changes thereto, together with any other items stipulated as being specifically included.

Contractor
One who undertakes responsibility for performance of construction work, including the provision of labor and materials, in accordance with plans and specifications and under a contract specifying cost and schedule for completion of the work; the person or organization responsible for performing the work, and identified as such in the owner-contractor agreement.

Contractor's estimate
1. A forecast of construction cost, as opposed to a firm proposal, prepared by a contractor for a project or a portion thereof.
2. A term sometimes used to denote a contractor's application or request for a progress payment.

Contractor's liability insurance
Insurance purchased and maintained by the contractor to protect him or her from specified claims which may arise out of or result from his operations under the contract, whether such operations be by himself or by any subcontractor or by anyone directly or indirectly employed by any of them, or by anyone whose acts any of them may be liable.

Curtain Wall
A wall that "hangs" on a structural frame.

Design Development
In this phase, the architect prepares (from the approved schematic design studies) for approval by the owner the drawings and other documents to fix and describe the size and character of the entire project as to structural, mechanical, and electrical systems, materials and such other essentials as my be appropriate; the architect also submits to the owner a further statement of probable construction cost.

Design Team
A group of design professionals from diverse disciplines working together to solve architectural opportunities. Architect, Mechanical Engineer, Lighting Consultant, etc.

Deregulation
Policy of FCC (and other government agencies) after the mid-1970s to remove existing regulations and rely on market forces such as competition for control of potential excesses.

Diffuser
A device commonly put on the bottom or sides of a luminaire to direct or spread the light from a source. It is used to control the brightness of the source and in many cases the direction of light emitted by the luminaire.

Direct Lighting
Lighting by luminaries distributing 90 to 100 percent of the emitted light in the general direction of the surface to be illuminated. The term usually refers to light emitted in a downward direction.

Elevation
A drawing or design that represents an interior or exterior view of the structure as being projected geometrically on a vertical plane parallel to one of its sides.

Energy Management System
An integrated group of products that regulate energy usage in a building. It may be a load control, an environmental control system, or a combination of the two.

Environmental Control System
An integrated group of products that control the heating-cooling-ventilation equipment in a building.

Float Glass
A flat glass sheet possessing high quality, polished, smooth surfaces; fabricated by floating the formed sheet glass on a molten-metal surface at a temperature high enough for the glass surfaces to flow freely.

Floor-Area Ratio
The ratio between the total floor area (for all floors) of a building which is permitted by code to the area of the lot on which the building is constructed.

Fluorescent Lamp
A low-pressure mercury electric discharge lamp, tubular in shape, in which a fluorescing coating (phosphor) transforms ultraviolet energy into visible light.

Foam Insulation
Thermal insulation which is applied to the outside of concrete forms between studs and over the top; used in sufficient thickness, with an airtight seal, to retain the heat of hydration so that the concrete is maintained at the required temperature for proper setting in cold weather.

Framed Building
A type of building construction in which the loads are carried to the ground by a framework or columns, rather than through load-bearing walls.

Generator
A machine that converts mechanical power into electric power.

Heat-Absorbing Glass
A faintly blue-green plate or float glass, which absorbs 40 percent of the sun's infrared (heat) rays and approximately 25 percent of the visible rays that pass through it; must be exposed uniformly to sunlight (without irregular shadows) to avoid cracking due to non-uniform heating.

Heat Pump
A refrigeration system in which heat is taken from a heat source and given up to the conditioned space when heating is required and is extracted from the space and discharged to a heat sink when cooling is required-the process being reversible.

Heat Recovery
The extraction of heat from any heat source such as lights, engine exhaust, etc.

HID High-Intensity Discharge lighting
A lighting type which includes mercury-vapor, metal-halide, and high-pressure sodium light sources. Although low-pressure sodium lamps are not HID sources, they often are included in the HID category.

HVAC
Industry terminology for heating, ventilating, and air conditioning.

Indirect lighting
Lighting by luminaires distributing 90 to 100 percent of the light emitted upward.

Kilowatt
A measure of electric current and voltage equal to 1000W.

Lamp
A light source, commonly called a "bulb" or "tube."

Laser
An acronym for light amplification by stimulated emission of radiation. Any one of a number of devices that can convert incident electromagnetic radiation of mixed frequency (incoherent) energy to one or more very specific or discrete frequencies of highly amplified and coherent visible radiation.

Lens
A glass or plastic shield that covers the bottom, and sometimes the sides, of a luminaire to control the direction and brightness of the light.

Line of sight
Above the frequencies at which skywave is reliable, radio propagation is limited to about 125 percent of the distance to the optical horizon or line-of sight.

Logo
The name of an organization represented in a distinctive type design with or without other emblems or symbols. Also knows as a signature cut, sig cut or logotype.

Louver
A series of baffles arranged in a geometric pattern, used to shield a lamp from view at certain angles to avoid glare.

Luminaire
A complete lighting fixture including one or more lamps and a means for connection to a power source. May also include one or more ballasts and elements to position and protect the lamps and distribute their light.

MEP
Industry terminology for mechanical, electrical and plumbing, in reference to engineering and building systems.

Modulation
A radio signal generally consists of a carrier wave and one or two sidebands. Sophisticated systems such as single sideband do not strictly follow this pattern, but they are not used for broadcasting, except for televisions vestigial sideband.

Multimedia
An overall term for the convergence of audio, video and computer media in the home or for business presentations.

NAB
National Association of Broadcasters, based in Washington, D.C.

NABET
(National Association of Broadcast Employees and Technicians) Originally, NABET stood for National Association of Broadcast Engineers and Technicians; the change from "engineers" to "employees" marked the trend in many unions to represent a broad range of job categories in a given station.

PAR lamp
A reflector lamp, usually incandescent, with a thick glass envelope, the back interior side has a parabolic shape with reflective coating; used with a lensed front of the envelope to provide desired spread of the light beam.

Plan (also Plan View)
A drawing made to scale to represent the top view or a horizontal section of a structure, as a floor layout of a building

PBS
Public Broadcasting Service.

Programming
Refers to format or type of program (or genre) such as soap opera; the term may also refer to the specific organization of content of a particular show. A program stripped or across the board is scheduled at the same time each weekday.

Propagation
Radio waves have three major means of propagation, and the efficiency of each varies with the frequency of the wave. Groundwave, for example, which hugs and travels along the earth's surface, is good for long-distance communication–up to worldwide in some cases – particularly when the ground conductivity near the transmitter is high, as is the extreme case with salt water, on frequencies from ELF into the medium-wave standard (AM) broadcast band. From about the middle of the standard broadcast band through the shortwave band, to abut 30 MHz or even a little beyond, the most effective long range mode is skywave. The wavelengths are such that signals bounce off the ionized layers that surround the earth, the ionosphere, at between 50 and 250 miles of altitude, much as a flashlight beam will bounce off a mirror.

Quasi-optical
Space communication satellites use frequencies in this quasi-optical range because, although far away in distance, they have an unobstructed line of sight to the earth station antenna – over one-third of the globe.

Radiation, conduction, induction
Electricity can travel from one point to another in a variety of ways. Conduction requires a conductor, usually a piece of wire, to carry the current. However, something not specially prepared as the conductor can also serve, as, for example, the earth, salt water, or some other common circuit ground. Induction uses the principle that an object may be electrified, magnetized, or given an induced voltage by exposure to a magnetic field.

Reflector
A device used to redirect the light from a lamp or luminaire by the process of reflection.

Remote
A broadcast or part that originates from outside the studio.

Repeaters
Unattended transmitters used to repeat the signal of a parent station. Used in television (also "satellites") for locations without sufficient population to make a full-fledged station financially viable or, in FM radio or television, to fill in areas the parent station's transmitter and antenna cannot cover because of mountainous terrain, etc.

Schematic Design Phase
The first phase of the architect's basic services. In this phase, the architect consults with the owner to ascertain the requirements of the project and prepares schematic design studies consisting of drawings and other documents illustrating the scale and relationship of the project components for approval by the owner. The architect also submits to the owner a statement of probable construction cost.

Sconce
An electric lamp, which is designed and fabricated for mounting on a wall.

Section
A representation of the structure as it would appear if cut by a plane, showing its internal structure and construction.

Soffit
The underside of an architectural feature, as a beam, arch, ceiling, vault, or cornice.

Staging
The temporary platform for workers and the materials they use in building erection; a scaffold.

Talent
A generic term referring to a person or persons appearing on radio or television as actor, announcer, singer, performer, on-air news reporter, and so forth.

Telecommunications
Any transmission, emission, or reception of signs, signals, writing images, and sounds or intelligence of any nature by wire, radio, visual, or other electromagnetic systems of communication. An implication of the first part of the word (tele- = far, distant) is that the communication takes place over a substantial distance.

Transmitter
A device for radiating signals that might be received at a distant location. (The term is also used for the portion of a telephone that is spoken into.) It is fed or controlled by a microphone or other speech input equipment, or a telegraph key, or some other source signal, and feeds to an antenna a composite signal that usually consists of a carrier wave, modulated by (has superimposed on it) the intelligence that one desires to transmit or send.

Voltage
A measure of electromotive force or the pressure of electricity

Watt
A unit used to measure power consumption of 1 amp under pressure of 1 volt.

Waves, propagation, frequency, wavelength
All electromagnetic waves or electromagnetic energies travel at 30,000 kilometers (roughly 186,300 miles) per second in free space, and a fraction slower in wire or other materials. What distinguishes these waves or parts of the electromagnetic spectrum–radio, infrared, visible light, ultraviolet, X-rays– from one another is their length, the actual distance from crest to crest or through to through.

Glosary Credits:

Dictionary of Architecture and Construction. Cyril M. Harris, Editor. 1975, McGraw-Hill, Inc., New York.

Stay Tuned: A History of American Broadcasting, Third Edition. Christopher H. Sterling and John Michael Kittross. 2002, Lawrence Erlbaum Associates, Mahwah, N.J. and London.

Air Studio
CBS Radio
Baltimore, Maryland
Bloomfield & Associates, Architects
Photographer: © Jeffrey Totaro/Esto